LA CUCINA
ITALIANA

SUPER

SEAFOOD

LA CUCINA ITALIANA

SUPER

SEAFOOD

Edited by Judith Ferguson

PRION

Published in the United Kingdom by
PRION,
an imprint of Multimedia Books Limited
32-34 Gordon House Road, London NW5 1LP

Exclusive distribution in the USA by
Smithmark Publishers Inc
16 East 32nd Street, New York, NY 10016

Editor: Judith Ferguson
Designer: Megra Mitchell
Production: Hugh Allan

Original recipes and pictures copyright © NEPI
La Cucina Italiana, **Via Mascheroni,**
1-20123 Milan
English translation and compilation copyright
© Multimedia Books Limited 1987, 1993

ISBN 1-85375-034-4

10 9 8 7 6 5 4 3 2

Printed in Italy by New Interlitho

CONTENTS

ANTIPASTI

In Italy, a meal always begins with either a plate of hot or cold "nibbles" or a bowl of sustaining soup. In the pages that follow, we offer a wonderful selection based on fish and seafood, including such dishes as an instant Crabmeat Salad, Seafood Soufflé, an elegant party piece, a simple Mussel Soup and a classic Rich Fish Soup.

& SOUPS

Smoked salmon domes (above);
terrine of sole (right, opposite)

Smoked Salmon Domes

Cupolette di salmone

To serve 8

8 slices of white bread

9oz smoked salmon, sliced

¼lb Belgian endive

¾ cup button mushrooms

2oz celery heart

juice of 1 lemon

1 tablespoon white-wine vinegar

¼ cup mayonnaise, plus extra for decorating

¼ cup heavy cream

Preparation time: about 30 minutes, plus chilling

Use 8 ramekins, molds or small bowls, about 3¼ inches in diameter. With a medium cookie cutter, cut out 8 circles from the bread. Line the molds first with plastic wrap leaving an overhang, then with the smoked salmon.

Trim the vegetables, rinse under running water and drain well. Dice finely and place in a bowl. Season with salt and pepper, lemon juice and vinegar and mix well, then add the mayonnaise. Whip the cream and fold it in gently.

Divide the mixture between the molds, cover each one with a circle of bread, then fold over the overhanging plastic wrap and seal it. Chill the molds in the refrigerator for at least 3 hours.

Just before serving, invert the molds on a large serving plate. Peel off the plastic wrap, then garnish each with mayonnaise. Garnish as you wish. (We arranged wafer-thin slices of cucumber between the domes and topped them with small pieces of celery.)

Terrine of Sole

Terrina da sogliole

To serve 6

11oz sole fillets

2 egg whites

a pinch of paprika

1¼ cups whipping cream

⅓ cup pistachio nuts, shelled and skinned

a small bunch watercress

12 slices smoked salmon, about 7oz

butter for greasing

olive oil and toast for serving

Preparation and cooking time: about 1 hour 20 minutes

Rinse and thoroughly dry the sole fillets. Chop them finely and rub through a coarse strainer to make a very smooth puree.

Place the puree in a bowl and, using a wooden spoon, gradually beat in the egg whites, a little at a time, adding salt to taste and a pinch of paprika. Stand the bowl in a bowl of ice and continue to beat the puree (you can use an electric beater), adding the cream in a steady stream until the mixture is smooth and aerated.

Chop the pistachios. Trim, wash and chop the watercress, then mix it and the pistachios into the fish mixture. Generously butter a 4½-cup ovenproof pâté dish or bread pan, then line it with the smoked salmon slices, leaving the ends overhanging. Spoon in the sole mixture and level the surface. Fold the smoked salmon over the top.

Butter a sheet of oil and cover the dish or pan with it, sealing the edges tightly. Stand the dish in a *bain-marie* half filled with boiling water and cook in the oven at 375°F for 30 minutes. Remove and leave to stand for 10 minutes before turning out.

This can be served hot or cool. Either way, drizzle over some olive oil and serve with toast.

Mussels with a Sea Tang

Cozze al Sapore di Mare

To serve 6

6½lb fresh mussels

4-6 shallots

½ celery heart

1½ cups mushrooms

a handful of parsley

1 tbsp chopped chives

2 tbsp butter

⅝ cup dry white wine

nutmeg

⅓ tsp cornstarch

a few drops lemon juice

Preparation and cooking time: about 1½ hours

Scrape the mussels with a small knife under running water, then leave them in a bowl of salted cold water for at least 30 minutes. Meanwhile, finely chop the shallots with the celery, mushrooms and a handful of parsley. Add the finely chopped chives and fry in 2 tablespoons of butter, taking care not to let the ingredients brown. Then put the mussels into the pan, pour in the wine, season generously with freshly ground black pepper and a little grated nutmeg. Cover the pan and allow the mussels to open over a high heat, shaking the pan from time to time.

Remove from the heat as soon as the mussels have opened. Take the mussels from their shells and place on a serving dish. Filter the liquid from the pan through a cheesecloth, then heat the liquid until it has reduced by half. Add the rest of the butter, softened, in small pieces. Dissolve the cornstarch in 2 or 3 tablespoons of cold water and a few drops of lemon juice and add this too. Simmer gently for a few seconds then pour over the mussels and sprinkle generously with chopped parsley. Serve immediately, garnishing the dish to taste.

Baked Mussels

Teglia di cozze

To serve 4–6

2lb mussels

olive oil

1 garlic clove, chopped

7oz frozen puff pastry dough, thawed

10 anchovy fillets

1 egg

3 slices white bread

1 small bunch fresh parsley

flour for dusting

Preparation and cooking time: about 40 minutes, plus thawing the dough

Preheat the oven to 200°F. Thoroughly scrub the mussels, removing the beards and any impurities; discard any that are open. Wash the mussels and place in a small saucepan with 4 tablespoons olive oil and the garlic. Cover and set over high heat until the mussels have opened. (Discard any that are still closed.) Remove the top shell from the mussels, leaving them on the half shell. Now divide the prepared mussels into two equal portions.

Roll out the dough on a lightly floured surface and, using a cookie cutter or a sharp knife, cut out enough teardrop shapes to cover half the mussels.

On half of the mussels, first lay a piece of anchovy, then a dough teardrop. Press the edges of the dough firmly onto the shells with your fingertips. Lightly beat the egg and brush it over the dough covers.

Crumble the bread and rub it through a strainer. Place the bread crumbs in a bowl and mix in the finely chopped parsley and a pinch of salt.

Then cover the remaining mussels with this mixture.

Arrange the mussels in rows in a baking dish, alternating the dough-covered and crumb-covered mussels. Trickle a little olive oil over the latter, then bake in the oven for about 15 minutes. Serve the mussels piping hot, straight from the oven.

Mussels with a sea tang (left, opposite); *baked mussels* (below)

Seafood Soufflé

Sformato Marino

To serve 8

1¼ lb cod fillets

1¾ cups ripe tomatoes

1 large onion

⅓ cup black olives, stoned and chopped

⅓ cup fresh breadcrumbs

⅓ cup butter

4 eggs

garlic

fresh basil

Preparation and cooking time: 1½ hours plus any defrosting time and soufflé cooling

1) Slice the cod fillets with a sharp knife. Lay them on a dish previously rubbed with garlic. Cover the cod with basil.

2) Bring to the boil a medium sized pan of salted water. Clean the tomatoes and drop them into the boiling water. Cook for two minutes and remove with a draining spoon.
Peel and finely chop the tomatoes and the onion. Melt 4 tablespoons of butter in a fry pan, add the chopped onion and fry gently.

3) Stir in the chopped tomatoes.

4) Stir in the cod. Season with salt and pepper and cook for 15 minutes, stirring occasionally.

5) Remove from the heat and add the olives and the breadcrumbs.

6) Add the eggs. Stir well and leave for a few minutes.

7) Meanwhile, grease a 10 x 8 inch ovenproof dish and pour in the mixture.

Cook in a *bain-marie* (**8** and **9**) for 1 hour in the oven at 375°F.

8) Pour some hot water into another larger oval pan.

9) . . . and immerse the smaller pan in it.
When cooked leave to cool and then turn out on to a serving dish. Garnish with finely sliced cucumber and radishes.

1

2

3

4

5

6

7

8

9

Shrimp in Aspic
Aspic di gamberetti

To serve 6

¾lb fresh uncooked shrimp

lemon juice

1 envelope powdered gelatin

1 small bunch parsley

pieces of red pepper in vinegar

4 hard-boiled egg yolks

6 tbsp mayonnaise

Worcestershire sauce

Preparation and cooking time: about 40 minutes, plus setting

Shell the shrimp and cook in a pan of salted water, acidulated with a little lemon juice. Drain and leave to cool.

Meanwhile, prepare the gelatin according to the directions on the package. Gently heat it and spoon a little into the bottom of 6 ramekins. Then, using a toothpick, arrange a shrimp, a parsley sprig and a small triangle of red pepper in each ramekin.

Rub the four egg yolks through a strainer into a bowl. Add the mayonnaise and 4 drops of Worcestershire sauce and mix well.

Chop all the remaining shrimp and mix them into the egg mixture. Rinse and finely chop the remaining parsley leaves and add to the mixture, with a pinch of salt and pepper. Put the mixture into a pastry bag with a flexible nozzle and pipe it into the ramekins.

Fill the ramekins almost to the top with the remaining gelatin and place in the refrigerator for at least 6 hours before serving. Remove the aspics from the refrigerator and unmold onto a plate, and garnish as you wish.

Crabmeat Salad
Insalata di polpa di granchio

To serve 6

7oz mixed salad leaves, such as lettuce heart, escarole, radicchio, mâche

11oz canned crabmeat

2 eggs

1 small bunch fresh parsley, finely chopped

½ tsp capers

juice of 1 lemon, strained

extra-virgin olive oil

grated nutmeg

Preparation and cooking time: about 20 minutes

Trim and rinse the salad leaves, then dry well and place in a salad bowl. Flake the crabmeat and remove any cartilages. Arrange the crab on the prepared salad leaves.

In a saucepan of cold water, place the eggs. Bring to a boil and hard-boil them for 8 minutes. Keep the whites for another use and rub the yolks through a strainer. Sprinkle them over the salad, together with the chopped parsley and the well-drained capers.

Now prepare the dressing. In a bowl, mix ½ teaspoon salt with the lemon juice, then incorporate about 6 tablespoons olive oil. Season with pepper and a pinch of nutmeg and pour the dressing over the salad. Toss just before serving.

You could also serve this appetizer on individual plates. Arrange the crabmeat in the center and surround it with the salad leaves.

Shrimp in aspic (far left, opposite); crabmeat salad (left)

Fish Mousses

Spumette di pesce

To serve 6

9oz small squid

1 medium onion

2 tbsp olive oil

¼ cup tomato passata or pureed tomatoes

1lb sole fillets, skinned and roughly chopped

2 eggs

scant ⅔ cup whipping cream

butter for greasing

Preparation and cooking time: about 45 minutes

Preheat the oven to 400°F. Clean the squid, rinse under running water, drain and dry. Finely dice the body sacs.

Slice the onion very thinly, then sweat in a small saucepan with the olive oil. Add the diced squid and cook for 3–4 minutes, then add the tomato passata. Season and cook the squid, uncovered, for about 15 minutes.

Meanwhile, puree the sole in a food processor or blender. Transfer to a bowl and break in the eggs. Using a wooden spoon, mix the puree, adding the cream to soften it. Season to taste and mix thoroughly.

Grease 6 ramekins with butter and place 1–2 tablespoons of sole mixture in each, spreading it out and making a hollow in the center with the back of a spoon. Fill these small cavities with the squid mixture, then fill up the ramekins with the remaining sole puree. Smooth over the surface, then stand the ramekins in a baking dish or on a cookie sheet and cook in the oven for about 20 minutes.

Remove the mousses from the oven as soon as they are cooked. Leave to rest for 5 minutes, then unmold them onto a large, warmed plate. Garnish if you wish with mâche and a few thin radish slices.

Melon Sorbet with Shrimp

Sorbetto di melone con gamberetti

To serve 6

1 medium melon

juice of ½ lemon

Worcestershire sauce

9oz uncooked shrimp, shelled

¼ cup dry white wine

1 firm, very ripe tomato

9 fresh basil leaves

3 tbsp olive oil

½ cucumber

6 cooked green beans

Preparation and cooking time: about 40 minutes

Halve the melon and discard the seeds, then scoop all the flesh into a blender and puree for 1 minute, or a little longer, until very smooth.

Transfer the puree to a bowl with the lemon juice, a few drops of Worcestershire sauce and 1½ cups water. Mix well, then chill in the refrigerator.

Cook the shrimp in a little boiling salted water and the wine for about 4 minutes. Drain and leave to cool. Dip the tomato briefly in boiling water, then quickly peel it. Remove the seeds and core and cut into strips, then cut the strips in half. Put the shrimp and tomato in a bowl and season with salt, pepper, three torn basil leaves and 3 tablespoons of olive oil. Mix gently, cover and leave to chill in the refrigerator.

Meanwhile, place the well-chilled melon puree in a *sorbetière* and churn according to the directions. When the sorbet is ready, place two or three scoops in ready chilled bowls. Divide the shrimp and tomato salad between the bowls and decorate with basil leaves, cucumber slices and green beans. Serve immediately.

Squid Stuffed with Smoked Salmon

Calamari al salmone

To serve 6

1 potato, about ¼lb

20 baby squid of equal size, about 1½lb

juice of ½ lemon

¼lb smoked salmon

4 tbsp butter, diced and softened

3 tbsp mayonnaise

6 slices white bread

6 ripe olives

½ cup cucumber slices

Preparation and cooking time: about 1 hour 15 minutes

Wash and boil the potato, then peel it and leave to cool. Meanwhile, clean the squid, discarding the cartilages and eyes. Rinse carefully and place in cold, lightly salted water with the lemon juice. Bring to a boil, then simmer until tender. Drain and leave to cool.

To make the stuffing, chop the smoked salmon and puree very finely in a food processor or blender. Mash the potato and place in a bowl. Mix in the salmon and diced, softened butter until perfectly smooth. Add the mayonnaise, beat it in, taste and add salt if necessary.

With a serrated knife, trim off the crusts from the bread, then cut the bread diagonally into triangles. Pit the olives and halve them lengthwise. Rinse the cucumber and slice very thinly. Using a cookie cutter, cut a hole ⅛ inch in diameter in the middle of each cucumber slice. Fill a waterproof pastry bag with some of the stuffing mixture and fill the squid, tying the openings with their tentacles or thread.

Pipe the remaining stuffing onto the center of the bread triangles. Top with a slice of cucumber and press down

lightly, then decorate with a slice of olive. Place a cucumber slice in the middle of a serving plate and arrange 8 stuffed squid in a rosette around it. Alternate the remaining squid and the bread triangles around the edge. Keep cool until ready to serve.

Tuna Delight

Delizia di Tonno

To serve 6

1 envelope gelatin (to make 2¼ cups)

1 tbsp lemon juice

1 egg

12oz canned tuna

1½ tbsp capers

4 anchovy fillets in oil

Worcestershire sauce

a little oil

a few leaves chicory

1 red bell pepper, cut into strips

Preparation and cooking time: about 1 hour

Dissolve the gelatin in 1¾ cups of warm water and add a tablespoon of lemon juice. Hard-boil the egg, shell and chop it and blend with the well-drained tuna, the drained capers, the anchovy fillets, a dash of Worcestershire sauce and the gelatin. Blend gently for a couple of minutes.

Oil a 3 cup fluted mold and pour in the tuna mixture. Place the mold in the freezer and allow the mixture to set. Turn out, slice it and arrange on a large plate. Garnish with strips of red bell pepper and sprigs of chicory. Serve.

Fish mousses (far left, opposite); tuna delight (left)

Meringue-topped Seashells

Conchiglie meringate

To serve 6

4 trout fillets

4 sole fillets

12 small clams in their shells

3oz leek

2 tbsp butter

¼ cup dry white wine

finely chopped fresh parsley

3 egg whites

grated nutmeg

2 tbsp grated Parmesan cheese

ground ginger

For the cooking and presentation: coarse sea salt and 6 scallop shells or small, shallow ramekins

Preparation and cooking time: about 45 minutes

Rinse and dry the fish and cut into small pieces. Clean the clams, removing any beards or impurities. Do not use any that are open. Open the clams and take them out of the shells.

Trim, wash and slice the leek. Place in a skillet with the butter and cook over high heat until tender.

Add all the pieces of fish and seal on both sides for 3 minutes, then add the clams. Pour in the white wine and cook until it has evaporated, then sprinkle a handful of chopped parsley over and a pinch of salt and pepper.

Make a bed of coarse sea salt in the bottom of a rectangular baking dish and arrange the scallop shells or ramekins on it. Fill the shells with the fish mixture.

Beat the egg whites with a pinch of salt until very stiff, then season them with a little nutmeg, the Parmesan cheese, a pinch of ginger and a little chopped parsley.

Put the prepared egg whites into a pastry bag with a plain nozzle, and pipe the meringue over the shells to cover them completely. Place under a hot broiler until the meringue is nicely browned. Serve immediately.

Creamed Smoked
Salmon Tartlets

Tartellette alla crema d'uovo e salmone

To serve 4–6

2oz smoked salmon

1 small bunch fresh parsley

5 eggs

scant ⅔ cup whipping cream

tomato catsup

For the pastry:

1¾ cups flour, plus extra for dusting

½ cup butter, diced and softened, plus extra for greasing

1 egg

paprika

Preparation and cooking time: about 1½ hours

To make the pastry dough, put the flour on a work surface. Make a well in the center and put in a pinch of salt and the softened butter. Work quickly until the ingredients are blended, then make a well again. Put the egg and 3 tablespoons cold water into the center. Add a pinch of paprika, then work quickly into a smooth dough. Shape it into a ball, cover with plastic wrap and leave to rest in the refrigerator for about 30 minutes, or even longer.

Meanwhile, preheat the oven to 400°F. Butter and flour sixteen 2-inch round tartlet pans with fluted edges. On the lightly floured work surface, roll out the dough to a thickness of ½ inch, prick with a fork then, using a plain round 2½-inch cookie cutter, cut out sixteen circles (re-roll and cut the trimmings). Line the tartlet pans with the dough circles, pressing them in firmly at the edges. Line with foil and beans, place all pans on a cookie sheet and bake blind in the preheated oven for 20 minutes.

Meanwhile, chop the smoked salmon

Creamed smoked salmon tartlets

and chop the parsley separately. In a saucepan, beat the eggs, then stir in the cream and season with salt. Place the saucepan either over another saucepan of simmering water on the stove or over very low heat and, stirring continuously with a wire whisk, beat the eggs until almost set and very creamy. Take the pan off the heat and mix in the chopped smoked salmon and parsley.

Take the tartlet shells out of the oven, unmold them and fill with the salmon cream. Garnish with a dollop of catsup in the center of each one. If you wish, garnish with parsley leaves. Place the tartlets on a serving dish and serve them tepid, so the pastry does not become soggy.

Scallops with Salmon Trout

Capesante salmonate

To serve 6

½lb salmon trout fillets

scant ⅔ cup light cream

6 large scallops in their shells

1 shallot, peeled and finely chopped

olive oil

¼ cup dry vermouth

1 slice white bread, crumbed

butter

Preparation and cooking time: about 40 minutes

Preheat the oven to 400°F. Make sure there are no bones in the trout fillets, then chop them very finely. Transfer to a food processor and puree at full speed for a few seconds, then mix in the cream and season to taste.

Open the scallops and keep the bottom shells. In a skillet, sweat the shallot with 2 tablespoons of olive oil until soft. Add the scallops, season and cook briefly until lightly colored. Remove the scallops from the pan and add the vermouth. Reduce the sauce until it has almost completely evaporated, then return the scallops to the pan to glaze them. Now turn off the heat.

Divide the salmon trout puree between the scallop shells and top each with a glazed scallop. Sprinkle the scallops with bread crumbs and dot with flakes of butter. Cook in the preheated oven for about 7 minutes, removing the scallops as soon as they are well browned.

Arrange on a serving plate and garnish as you wish. To keep the shells standing firm, we arranged them on a bed of coarse sea salt. We garnished the plate with lemon wedges, cucumber slices and lettuce leaves.

Scallops with salmon trout

Shrimp Soup Under a Pastry Lid

Zuppette di gamberi in crosta

To serve 2

11oz uncooked shrimp, unshelled

⅓ cup finely chopped shallots

⅓ cup finely chopped leeks

2 tbsp olive oil

1 bay leaf

brandy

dry white wine

2 tbsp butter, softened

1½ tbsp flour

scant ⅔ cup whipping cream

For the pastry lids:

7oz frozen puff pastry dough, thawed

1 egg, beaten

Preparation and cooking time: about 1 hour 15 minutes

Thoroughly rinse the shrimp under cold running water. Sweat the finely chopped shallots and leeks in a saucepan with the olive oil and bay leaf until tender. Add the shrimp, season and cook for 2–3 minutes, until the shrimp turn pink.

Pour in a small glass of brandy and flame it, or, if you prefer, evaporate the liquid over very fierce heat. Sprinkle a little white wine over the shrimp, then pour 1¾ cups cold water over and boil for about 20 minutes.

Meanwhile, preheat the oven to 350°F. Take the soup off the heat and take out the shrimp. Remove the heads and shells and set aside the flesh. Return the soup to the heat and add the shrimp heads and shells. Mash together the softened butter and flour, then mix into the soup and cook for about 10 minutes longer.

Pass the soup through a food mill, using the finest disk, or a fine-meshed strainer. Cut up the shrimp bodies and add them to the soup, together with the whipping cream, and cook for another 10 minutes, until the soup thickens to

the consistency of heavy cream. Divide it between two ovenproof soup bowls.

Roll out the thawed dough on a lightly floured work surface into a thin rectangle. Cut out two circles slightly larger than the diameter of the two ovenproof soup bowls. Brush the edges with a little beaten egg, then cover the filled bowls with the dough circles, pressing the edges lightly against the sides of the bowls. Brush the lids with a little egg, then bake in the oven for about 20 minutes. Serve the soup straight from the oven.

Fish Soup with Anchovy

Zuppa "Marechiaro"

To serve 4

4 small striped mullet

4 small scorpion fish

¾–1lb cleaned skate

8 crayfish

12 cleaned baby cuttlefish

4 anchovy fillets

3 garlic cloves

olive oil

1 small onion

1 carrot

a few sprigs parsley

1lb ripe tomatoes

1 bay leaf

white wine

⅔ cup good fish stock

4 slices home-made bread

Preparation and cooking time: about 1½ hours

Clean and scale the mullet and scorpion fish, cut off the fins, then wash and drain them well.

Chop the skate and wash the crayfish and cuttlefish. Slightly crush 2 large garlic cloves and place them in a large saucepan with the anchovy fillets and 6 tablespoons of oil. Fry gently and mash the anchovies. Discard the garlic and add the onion and carrot, finely chopped with a sprig of parsley; soften for a few

minutes, then add the cuttlefish and cook for about 10 minutes.

Meanwhile peel and purée the tomatoes and add them to the pan. Season with salt, pepper, and a small bay leaf. Simmer for about 20 minutes with the pan covered, then add the mullet, the scorpion fish and the pieces of skate in a single layer. Moisten with the white wine and pour in the fish stock.

Shake the saucepan gently and cook for 15 minutes, then add the crayfish and keep on the heat for a further 5 minutes.

Hake-flavored Pasta Soup

Minestra del Marinaio

To serve 4

2 small ripe tomatoes

a bunch of fresh parsley

1 garlic clove

olive oil

1 fresh hake weighing about 1lb

1lb small pasta shells (conchigliette)

Preparation and cooking time: about 40 minutes

Wash the tomatoes and blanch them for a few minutes in lightly salted boiling water. Skin them, cut in half and remove the seeds, then chop coarsely (they should remain in pieces). Rinse and dry the parsley and coarsely chop this too. Peel the garlic, remove the green shoot and slice finely.

Heat a large saucepan containing the tomatoes, half the parsley, the garlic, a tablespoon of olive oil and about 4 pints of water. Season with a pinch of salt and a little freshly ground pepper. Bring to the boil and simmer for about 10 minutes. Meanwhile clean and rinse the fish. Remove the tail and fins and clean the hake. Wash thoroughly then add to the boiling liquid.

Cook for about 10 minutes then very carefully remove the fish from the soup. Pour in the pasta, cook until it is *al dente* and remove the pan from the heat. Add the remaining parsley, mix and pour into a soup tureen. Serve at once. (The hake is not eaten with the soup. It can be served as a second course dressed with olive oil and strained lemon juice.)

Swordfish and Bell Pepper Soup

Zuppetta di spada e peperoni

To serve 6

2 bouillon cubes

1 medium onion

3 tbsp olive oil

1 garlic clove

1 each small red and yellow bell peppers

fresh basil leaves

¾lb swordfish steaks, diced

Preparation and cooking time: about 30 minutes

Bring about 4½ cups water to a boil with the bouillon cubes. Chop the onion and sweat in a saucepan with the olive oil and garlic. Peel, core and dice the peppers and add them to the onion, with 3 or 4 basil leaves.

After about 10 minutes, add the diced swordfish. Increase the heat to high and cook for 2 minutes, then pour in the boiling stock. Remove the basil leaves, lower the heat and simmer for 5 minutes longer.

Taste the soup, correct the seasoning and take the pan off the heat. Leave to stand for 2–3 minutes before serving. If you like, place a slice of toasted French bread or a classic crouton in the bottom of each bowl before ladling in the soup.

Shrimp soup under a pastry lid (far left, opposite); swordfish and bell pepper soup (left, above)

Fish Soup Cooked in the Oven

Zuppa di Pesce, in Forno

To serve 4

4½lb mixed fish (red mullet, skate, dogfish, John Dory, gurnard, hake and dentex)

5-6 sprigs parsley

1 medium-sized onion

2 bay leaves

1 celery heart and a few leaves

2 garlic cloves

1-1¼lb ripe tomatoes

⅜ cup olive oil

½ cup dry white wine

4 slices bread

Preparation and cooking time: about 1½ hours

Gut and wash the fish; leave the smaller ones whole and cut the others in pieces, removing as many of the bones as possible and cutting off the heads. Place the heads in a saucepan with the bones and scraps, cover them with water, salt lightly, add a sprig of parsley, a quarter of the onion cut in slices and a bay leaf. Put the saucepan on the heat and let the stock simmer for about 30 minutes covered.

Preheat the oven to 400°F. In an ovenproof dish with a lid place the rest of the sliced onion, the celery heart and 4-5 finely chopped parsley sprigs, a whole garlic clove, a bay leaf and the tomatoes, chopped and puréed through the food processor using the fine disk. Arrange the fish on top of the vegetables, pour in the oil, salt and pepper lightly and then moisten with the white wine and the fish stock strained carefully through a fine cloth.

Cover the pan and place it in the oven for about 30 minutes. Toast the slices of bread in the oven; when golden brown brush them with a garlic clove and place them in 4 soup plates. Pour over the soup, sprinkle each portion with a few finely chopped celery leaves and a few drops of olive oil, then serve.

Rich Fish Soup

Zuppa di Pesce, Ricca

To serve 6

6½lb mixed fish (scorpion fish, gurnard, mullet, John Dory, skate)

1-1¼lb squid and small octopus

1-1¼lb shrimp and jumbo shrimp

2¼ cups dry white wine

¾ cup olive oil

3 garlic cloves

6 anchovy fillets

1 small piece red chili pepper

2 bunches parsley

6 basil leaves

1-1¼lb ripe tomatoes, chopped and seeded

12 mussels

6 razor-shell clams

oregano

6 slices home-made bread toasted in the oven

Preparation and cooking time: about 2 hours

Gut and wash the fish thoroughly, cut off the heads and fillet the larger ones. Cut the others into regular pieces, wash again and leave to drain. Clean the squid and octopus, removing the heads, the hard beaks and the viscera, then wash several times in plenty of water. Wash the shrimp.

Heat in a large saucepan the white wine, 4½ cups of water and all the fish heads and bones. Salt lightly and simmer on a very low heat for about 1 hour. Meanwhile, in ⅜ cup of oil in a small saucepan brown 3 crushed garlic cloves and dissolve the anchovy fillets. Add the shrimp, salt lightly, pepper and leave to brown for about 10 minutes, turning them often. Pour the mixture into the large saucepan containing the fish heads, add the piece of chili pepper and continue to cook, still over a very low heat.

Wash the parsley and basil and chop them finely. Heat about ⅜ cup of oil in a very large saucepan; as soon as it is hot add the tomatoes puréed through a food processor, salt lightly and cook until the sauce is thick. Place the squid and octopus in the pan and, after about 20 minutes, add the fish. Cover and cook over quite a high heat without stirring.

Strain the prepared stock through a fine cloth, discarding the heads; if you wish you can keep the shrimp and add the shelled meat to the soup. Pour the stock into the pan containing the fish and cook for another 10 minutes. Five minutes before removing the soup from the heat, add the washed mussels and razor-shell clams and season with the mixture of chopped parsley and basil and a pinch of oregano. Serve the soup with the toasted bread slices.

Shellfish Soup

Zuppa di Molluschi

To serve 4

4½lb mixed shellfish (mussels, clams, razor-shell clams, Venus clams)

8 slices home-made bread

about ¾ cup olive oil

3 garlic cloves

a small piece red chili pepper

2 tbsp ready-made tomato sauce

3 cups good fish stock

a few tender celery leaves

Preparation and cooking time: about 40 minutes plus 2 hours' soaking

Scrape the shells of the shellfish, holding them under cold running water, then place them all in a large bowl, cover with cold water and leave them undisturbed for about 2 hours. Then leave them to drain for a while to remove any sand.

Fry the slices of bread on both sides in ⅜ cup oil; while still hot brush them with a large halved garlic clove and arrange them in 4 soup bowls. Heat a large skillet with ⅜ cup of oil, 2 large lightly crushed garlic cloves and the chili pepper: fry lightly until the garlic and pepper have browned, then discard them. Place the shellfish in the pan, cover and keep on

the heat until all the shells have opened. Remove them, one by one, from the pan, detaching one half-shell and placing the other one containing the mussel or clam in a clean saucepan.

Strain through a fine cloth the liquid which the shellfish gave out during cooking and add it to the saucepan. Add 2 tablespoons of ready-made tomato sauce blended with the hot fish stock, shake the saucepan slightly and keep it on the heat for a few moments, then pour the soup over the bread slices. Sprinkle each portion with chopped celery leaves and a few drops of olive oil. Serve immediately.

Shellfish soup (top left)*; **fish soup with anchovy** (centre left, recipe on page 22)**; **rich fish soup** (top right)**; **baked fish soup** (bottom right)*

Clam and Angler-Fish Soup

Zuppa di Vongole e Pescatrice

To serve 4-6

¾lb "tail" of angler-fish, skin and bones removed

1 medium onion

1 large garlic clove

3 tbsp butter

3 tbsp olive oil

⅜ cup dry white wine

2 small tomatoes, peeled and puréed

2 fresh basil leaves

oregano

1 tbsp cornstarch

3½ pints fish stock

6oz frozen clams

3 slices white bread

Preparation and cooking time: about 1¼ hours

Dice the fish. Slice the onions very finely and cut the garlic clove in half. Fry the onion and garlic in 5 teaspoons of the butter and 3 tablespoons of olive oil until transparent. Add the diced fish and fry gently. Sprinkle with the white wine and allow the wine to evaporate before adding the puréed tomatoes. Season with 2 leaves of fresh basil, a pinch of oregano and plenty of pepper.

Dissolve a tablespoon of cornstarch in the fish stock and add to the pan with the rest of the stock. Stir well and bring to the boil. Lower the heat and simmer gently for about 20 minutes. Then blend the mixture until smooth. Stir in the frozen clams, replace the pan on the heat and bring back to the boil. Simmer for a further 10 minutes. Test and adjust the seasoning. Dice the bread and toss gently in the remaining butter until golden. Serve hot with the soup.

Mussel Soup

Zuppa di Cozze

To serve 4

50 large mussels

2 small garlic cloves

¼ cup olive oil

¾lb ripe tomatoes

2 fresh basil leaves

a few parsley sprigs

slices of toasted home-made bread

Preparation and cooking time: about 1 hour

Wash the mussels thoroughly under cold running water, and scrape them clean with a small knife. As they are ready, put them in a large skillet or saucepan over a moderate heat. As the shells open, remove them from the pan and extract the mussels, throwing away the shells. Divide the mussels among 4 individual bowls. Cover each bowl with a piece of wet wax paper and keep them hot by placing them in a low oven with the door open.

Strain the liquid from the mussels through a clean cloth. Remove the central green shoot from the garlic and put in a garlic crusher. Collect the crushed garlic in a skillet with the olive oil and fry gently for a few seconds. Put the tomatoes, washed and cut into pieces, through a food processor using the medium disk, and add to the garlic in the skillet.

Stir and add the basil leaves, salt and pepper. Simmer for about 10 minutes then stir in the liquid from the mussels and a sprig of parsley, coarsely chopped. Remove the basil leaves and continue simmering for 3-4 minutes. Check the seasoning and divide the sauce among the 4 bowls of mussels. Garnish each bowl with a sprig of parsley and serve with slices of toasted home-made bread.

PASTA, RISOTTOS

The "primi piatti" as it is called in Italy is the most *Italian* part of the meal, consisting as it does of pasta, rice (always the short-grain variety grown in the northern part of the country), or gnocchi, small lighter-than-air balls made from grains or potatoes usually served with a sauce. Here we offer a whole selection of traditional and new classics to continue the meal in style.

& GNOCCHI

Pasta Spirals with Squid

Fusilli calamari

To serve 6

12 small squid, about 1lb

1 small bunch fresh parsley

1 garlic clove

3 slices white bread

3 tbsp grated Parmesan cheese

olive oil

2 medium onions

1 cup dry white wine

1lb pasta spirals

Preparation and cooking time: about 1 hour

Preheat the oven to 190°F. Clean the squid; separate the heads from the body sacs and remove the cartilages and intestines from the sacs. Rinse the sacs, taking care not to tear them. Chop a good bunch of parsley with the squid heads and garlic and place in a bowl. Add the finely crumbled bread, the Parmesan, 1 tablespoon of olive oil and salt and pepper to taste. Mix this stuffing thoroughly, then fill the squid with it, closing the openings with wooden toothpicks or string.

Slice the onions very thinly. Heat 4 tablespoons of oil in a flameproof casserole, then put in the onions and sweat them until transparent. Add the squid and cook over high heat for several minutes, then pour in the white wine and a little water and season. Cover the dish with aluminum foil, transfer to the oven and cook for about 40 minutes.

When the squid are ready, cook the pasta spirals until they are *al dente*. Take the squid out of the baking dish and remove the toothpicks. Drain the pasta and tip it into the dish with the sauce. Toss the squid into the pasta, transfer to a serving dish, sprinkle with chopped parsley if you wish, and serve.

Pasta Shells "Sailor Style"

Conchiglie marinare

To serve 6

9oz jumbo uncooked shrimp

9oz cod fillets

olive oil

2 garlic cloves, lightly crushed

1 small bunch fresh parsley, chopped

½ cup dry white wine

1 cup tomato passata

1lb pasta shells

Preparation and cooking time: about 40 minutes

Remove and discard the shrimp shells. Cut the cod into ¼-inch slices. In a large skillet, heat 4 tablespoons of olive oil. Add the lightly crushed garlic and cook until well colored. Remove the garlic and put the shrimp and cod slices into the pan. Season and, over high heat, let the fish absorb the flavors for a few minutes. Add 1 tablespoon of chopped parsley, pour in the wine and let it evaporate.

As soon as the wine has evaporated from the sauce, add the tomato passata and ½ cup of water. Mix and simmer over low heat for 15 minutes.

Meanwhile, cook the pasta until it is *al dente*. Drain, and add it to the pan with the sauce. Toss well and transfer to a serving dish.

Pasta with Seafood Sauce

Trofie al sugo di mare

To serve 4–6

14oz crawfish

¼lb jumbo shrimp

1 large onion, peeled

1 small bunch fresh parsley

olive oil

⅔ cup dry white wine

⅔ cup tomato passata

2 shallots

¼ cup butter

1lb pasta spirals

Preparation and cooking time: about 1 hour

Carefully rinse the crawfish and shrimp, then shell them, reserving the shells. Using poultry shears, cut up the shells into tiny pieces. Slice the onion very thinly and finely chop half the parsley. Put 3 tablespoons of olive oil in a saucepan, add the onion, parsley and crustacean shells and color over high heat for 3–4 minutes, stirring continuously with a wooden spoon. Pour in half the white wine, let it evaporate, then add the tomato passata and 2½ cups cold water. Mix again, then bring up to the boiling point. Immediately lower the heat and simmer gently for 40 minutes. Check the sauce from time to time, and if it starts to dry out, add another glass of water. When the sauce is ready, tip it into a strainer, and press down hard on the shells.

Finely chop the shallots and sweat them in a skillet with 1 tablespoon of oil; add the shrimp and crawfish and color them lightly, stirring with a wooden spoon. Add the remaining wine and evaporate it. Season the strained sauce with salt and mix it with the shellfish. Bring to a boil and cook for 5 minutes. Pour the mixture into a blender and puree on full power for just 1–2 minutes.

Meanwhile, cook the pasta in boiling salted water until it is *al dente*. One minute before draining it, melt the butter in a skillet, add the remaining finely chopped parsley and soften it, then pour in the blended sauce and finally the drained pasta. Mix well so that the sauce goes right into the spirals and serve immediately.

Fish ravioli with cream and basil (left); pasta with seafood sauce (right)

Fish Ravioli with Cream and Basil

Ravioli di pesce con panna e basilico

To serve 4–6

For the pasta:

1¾ cups flour

2 eggs

olive oil

salt

For the filling:

11oz sole fillets

¼lb uncooked shrimp, shelled

2 egg yolks

3 tablespoons whipping cream

1 bunch fresh parsley, finely chopped

For the sauce:

1 bunch fresh basil

3 tablespoons butter

1 cup whipping cream

Preparation and cooking time: about 1½ hours

First prepare the pasta. Sift the flour onto a work surface and make a well. Add the eggs, a pinch of salt and ½ tablespoon of oil. Mix all the ingredients together, then knead the dough energetically until it becomes smooth and firm. Cover and leave to rest in the refrigerator for 30 minutes.

Meanwhile, prepare the filling. Very finely chop the sole fillets and shrimp and place in a bowl. Add the egg yolks, cream, the finely chopped parsley leaves, a few grindings of pepper and a

small pinch of salt.

If you have a pasta machine, roll out the dough into thin sheets. If you do not have a machine, carefully roll out the dough into large thin sheets, about ¼ inch thick and about 24 inches square. Spoon little heaps of the stuffing onto the lower half of each sheet, spacing them at regular intervals. Fold over the top half of each pasta sheet to cover the filling, pressing well to seal. Using a fluted pasta cutter or a sharp knife, cut out individual raviolis about 2-inches square.

Bring a large pan of water to a boil and, when it is boiling, add salt. Put in a few ravioli at a time and cook until they are *al dente* and float to the surface; repeat until all the ravioli have been cooked.

Chop the basil leaves and sweat in a skillet with the butter. Add the cream and bring to a boil. Drain the ravioli, pour the sauce over them, mix and serve at once.

Tagliatelle with Clams and Zucchini

Tagliatelle con vongole e zucchine

To serve 4

14oz clams

1 garlic clove

olive oil

¾lb tagliatelle

fresh basil leaves

fresh sage leaves

2 cups sliced zucchini

Preparation and cooking time: about 20 minutes

Rinse the clams in several changes of water, then leave them to soak in fresh water for at least 2 hours to remove all traces of sand. Split the garlic clove and lightly crush it, using the flat edge of a knife. Place in a large skillet with 1 tablespoon of olive oil and heat, then add the clams.

Meanwhile, bring a pan of water to a boil for the tagliatelle.

In another shallow pan, heat 3 tablespoons of olive oil, flavor with a few basil and sage leaves, then add the zucchini. Season and sauté over very high heat. Transfer the open clams still in their shells from the other pan, discarding any that are not open, and strain all their cooking juices over. Leave to simmer while you cook the tagliatelle until it is *al dente*, then drain it. Pour the pasta into the sauce, shaking the pan vigorously to disperse the flavor, then transfer to a serving dish. Serve at once.

Pasta spirals with fresh anchovy sauce (top); tagliatelle with clams and zucchini (bottom)

Pasta Spirals with Fresh Anchovy Sauce
Fusilli alla pescatora

To serve 6

11oz fresh anchovies, cleaned and gutted

1¾ cups peeled and chopped tomatoes

1 garlic clove

fresh basil leaves

olive oil

1lb pasta spirals

finely chopped fresh parsley

Preparation and cooking time: about 30 minutes, plus 12 hours marinating

Remove the heads from the anchovies then rinse, drain well and chop them. Place in a bowl with the chopped tomatoes, the lightly crushed garlic and a few basil leaves. Season, then pour in 5 tablespoons olive oil. Cover the bowl with plastic wrap and leave to marinate in the refrigerator for at least 12 hours.

Just before serving, bring a large pan of salted water to a boil, and cook the pasta spirals until they are *al dente*. Drain, place in a serving dish, and mix in the anchovy sauce. Sprinkle with chopped parsley and serve.

Pasta Bows with Chicken and Shrimp
Farfalle al volo

To serve 6

1lb pasta bows

1 small chicken breast half

3 tablespoons butter

5oz shelled uncooked shrimp

½ cup diced cooked ham

1 ripe tomato, peeled

1 small bunch fresh parsley

Preparation and cooking time: about 15 minutes

Bring a large pan of water to a boil and, when it is boiling, add salt. Throw in the pasta bows and cook until they are *al dente*.

Meanwhile, cut the skinned chicken breast half into small dice and seal all over in a skillet with the butter. Rinse and wipe the shrimp, then slice them thinly. Season the chicken, then add the shrimp and ham to the pan and cook over low heat for about 5 minutes. Remove the seeds and core from the tomato and dice the flesh. Add this to the pan, together with a handful of chopped parsley.

Drain the pasta, put it in the skillet and mix well. Transfer to a serving dish and serve immediately.

Tagliatelle with Seafood
Tagliatelle alla Marinara

To serve 4

1¾ cups flour

2 eggs

olive oil

salt

For the sauce:

⅓ cup finely chopped onion

olive oil

9oz whiting or whitefish fillets, cut into bite-sized pieces

¼ cup shelled uncooked shrimp

¼ cup dry white wine

1 tablespoon tomato paste

1 × 14oz can chopped tomatoes, undrained

1 tablespoon finely chopped parsley

Preparation and cooking time: about 40 minutes, plus resting the pasta dough

First prepare the tagliatelle. Sift the flour onto a work surface and make a well. Break the eggs into the middle and add 1 tablespoon of olive oil and a pinch of salt. Mix with a fork until the eggs and flour are well combined, then work the dough with your hands until it is firm, but elastic. Wrap the dough in plastic wrap and leave to rest in the refrigerator for about 30 minutes.

Meanwhile, sweat the onion gently in a saucepan with 2 tablespoons of oil. As soon as the onion is soft, add the whiting or whitefish fillets and the shrimp. Seal the fish on both sides for a couple of minutes, then sprinkle with white wine. When the wine has evaporated, add the tomato paste and the chopped tomatoes and their juice. Season to taste, then cover the pan and simmer for about 35 minutes.

Fill a large pan with plenty of salted water and bring to a boil. Unwrap the pasta dough and, using a pasta machine, roll it out and cut it into tagliatelle. If you do not have a pasta machine, divide the dough into sections, roll out very thinly and then cut into strips. Cook in the boiling water until *al dente*. Drain and place in a serving dish. Pour all the sauce over, sprinkle with chopped parsley and serve at once, piping hot.

Pasta Spirals with Anchovies and Olives

Tortiglioni in marinata

To serve 6

4 ripe tomatoes, peeled

3oz rocket or other bitter salad leaves

6 anchovy fillets in oil, chopped

⅔ cup pitted olives, sliced

¼ cup olive oil

1lb pasta spirals

Preparation and cooking time: about 15 minutes

Remove the seeds and cores from the tomatoes, then dice the flesh and place it in a serving bowl. Rinse and dry the salad leaves, cut them into thin slivers and add to the tomatoes, together with the chopped anchovies, sliced olives and a pinch each of salt and pepper. Finally, mix in the oil, cover the bowl with plastic wrap and set aside to rest.

Cook the pasta until it is *al dente*, then drain it. Place it in a serving bowl and mix it well with the sauce.

Pasta Quills with Shellfish

Penne ai frutti di mare

To serve 4

1lb cockles or clams

14oz Queen scallops

14oz mussels

olive oil

1 garlic clove

1 shallot

½ leek

3 tbsp butter

1 tbsp chopped fresh herbs (parsley, sage, thyme, rosemary, marjoram)

4 tbsp dry white wine

¾lb short pasta quills

Preparation and cooking time: about 1 hour

Scrub the shellfish and wash in cold water to remove all traces of sand or beard. Discard any clams, scallops or mussels that are open. Heat 2 tablespoons of oil with the garlic in a saucepan, then add each type of shellfish separately and cook them until they open. (Discard any that do not open.) Set aside. Strain the mussel cooking juice and reserve it.

Meanwhile, chop the shallot and leek and sweat in the butter for 2 minutes. Add the shellfish and season with a pinch each of salt and pepper and the chopped herbs. Sprinkle the white wine over and evaporate it over high heat, then add ½ glass of the mussel juice. Reduce by about half.

Fill a large saucepan with plenty of salted water and bring to a boil for the pasta. Add the pasta and cook until *al dente*. Drain it, then add immediately to the sauce and, still over high heat, toss the pasta to flavor it well. Transfer to a serving dish and serve immediately.

Pasta Shells "Neptune"

Conchiglie "Nettuno"

To serve 6

14oz mussels

olive oil

2 garlic cloves

11oz small squid

2 medium onions

dry white wine

1 envelope powdered saffron

1 × 14oz can plum tomatoes, chopped

1 small bunch fresh parsley

1lb pasta shells

Pasta quills with shellfish (left); risotto with salmon trout (right)

Preparation and cooking time: about 45 minutes

Thoroughly rinse the mussels, scrubbing them to remove the beards and other impurities; discard any that are open. Place in a skillet with 2 tablespoons of olive oil and 1 clove of garlic. Cover and set over high heat until the mussels have opened (discard any that do not open). Take the pan off the heat and take the mussels out of their shells, keeping them warm. Strain any cooking liquid through a fine strainer and reserve it.

Clean the squid and remove the cartilages and the eyes. Wash them carefully, then cut the bodies into rings. Chop the onions and split the remaining garlic clove by pressing it with the flat edge of a knife. Sweat them until soft in a saucepan with 2 tablespoons of oil. Add the squid and cook over high heat for 1–2 minutes, stirring with a wooden spoon. Season lightly, lower the heat and continue to cook until all the liquid has evaporated. Pour in the wine and let it evaporate, then pour in the same amount of reserve mussel cooking liquid (top up with water if there isn't enough). Stir in the saffron, tomatoes without their juice, some coarsely chopped parsley and a pinch of salt and pepper.

Cook the pasta shells until they are *al dente* and drain them as soon as they are ready. Toss in the sauce, add the mussels and sprinkle with 1–2 tablespoons of finely chopped parsley. Serve immediately.

Risotto with Salmon Trout

Risotto saporito

To serve 4

1 shallot

olive oil

1½ cups short-grain rice, such as arborio

6 tbsp dry vermouth

3¾ cups hot stock (made from a cube, if necessary)

5oz salmon trout fillet

¼ cup light cream

1 tablespoon chopped fresh herbs (parsley, sage, rosemary, marjoram)

Preparation and cooking time: about 30 minutes

Peel and chop the shallot and sweat it in a saucepan with 2 tablespoons of olive oil. Add the rice and toast it over high heat for a few minutes, then sprinkle on the vermouth. When it has evaporated, continue to cook the rice, adding the hot stock, a little at a time, and stirring it frequently with a wooden spoon.

Remove any bones or skin from the salmon trout and cut the flesh into small pieces. Add these to the half-cooked rice. Finish cooking the rice until it is *al dente*, but still moist, which takes 20–25 minutes, then remove from the heat and stir in the cream to give it a rich texture. Season with salt and the chopped herbs. Cover the pan and leave the risotto to rest for 2–3 minutes. Transfer it to a serving dish and garnish as you wish.

Seafood Risotto

Risotto alla marinara

To serve 6

For the risotto:

5½ cups arborio rice

olive oil

1 medium onion, chopped

generous 2½ cups light stock (can be made with a cube)

butter for the mold

For the garnish:

14oz mussels

olive oil

2 garlic cloves

9oz small squid

5oz uncooked shrimp

oregano

1 tomato, peeled and chopped

Preparation and cooking time: about 1 hour

Cook the rice in the Italian way by sweating it gently in a little oil with the onion, then gradually adding the stock, waiting until one addition has been absorbed before adding another. It will take about 20 minutes to cook to *al dente*. Preheat the oven to 400°F.

Meanwhile, scrub the mussels, removing the beards and discarding any that are open. Put them in a saucepan with 2 tablespoons of olive oil and a lightly crushed clove of garlic. Set over high heat and, as soon as the mussels open, take them out of their shells and strain and reserve the cooking juices. Discard any that do not open. Clean the squid, removing the cartilages and eyes. Then separate the tentacles and bodies and cut into pieces. Shell the shrimp and chop them.

Heat 3 tablespoons olive oil and half a chopped garlic clove in a saucepan, add a grinding of pepper, oregano to taste and the squid tentacles and bodies. Add the tomato and, when the sauce is almost boiling, add the shrimp and mussels. Thin the sauce with the mussel juices, season with salt and boil for 3 minutes. Pour the sauce over the prepared risotto.

Butter a fish-shaped (or any other suitable shape) mold and fill with the seafood risotto. Stand the mold in a *bain-marie* and cook in the preheated oven for about 20 minutes. Leave to stand for 1 minute before unmolding onto a serving dish. Garnish as you wish, and serve immediately.

Potato Gnocchi with Shrimp

Gnocchi di patate agli scampi

To serve 6

For the gnocchi:

2lb floury potatoes

heaped 2½ cups flour, plus extra for dusting

1 egg

2 tbsp grated Parmesan cheese

grated nutmeg

For the sauce:

1lb uncooked jumbo shrimp

fresh sage leaves

fresh rosemary leaves

olive oil

dry white wine

⅔ cup whipping cream

1 cup tomato passata or pureed tomatoes

Preparation and cooking time: about 1½ hours

First, prepare the gnocchi. Scrub the potatoes, place them in a pan of cold water in their skins and cook for about 20 minutes, or until tender. Peel them and push through a potato ricer or a strainer directly onto a work surface. Mix in the flour, egg, Parmesan, a

pinch of salt and some freshly grated nutmeg. Work the mixture with your hands until you have a smooth, soft, pliable dough. Divide the dough into several pieces.

Lightly dust the work surface with flour and roll each piece of dough along the surface into a tube shape. Cut each tube into ¾-inch pieces. Press the gnocchi, one at a time, against the back of a fork or some other utensil to give them ridges, then, as soon as each one is ready, place it in a dish covered with a lightly floured dish towel.

To make the sauce, shell the shrimp, rinse well and cut in half. Chop a few sage leaves and rosemary leaves together and place them in a skillet with 5 tablespoons of olive oil. Heat, then immediately add the shrimp, season and cook over high heat for 2 minutes, stirring with a wooden spoon. Pour in a little white wine, let it evaporate, then add the cream and tomato passata. Mix again, bring to a boil and cook for about 4 minutes.

Meanwhile, bring a large pan of salted water to a boil. Add the gnocchi, a few at a time, lifting them out with a slotted spoon as soon as they rise to the surface. Drain and place in a deep, warmed serving dish. Pour the sauce over at once and serve.

Russian-style Spaghetti with Crab and Vodka

Spaghetti alla russa con granchio e vodka

To serve 4

---

1 small shallot

---

1 tbsp olive oil

6oz canned or frozen crabmeat

---

1 small bunch fresh parsley

¼ cup vodka

14oz spaghetti

---

4 tbsp butter, diced

Preparation and cooking time: about 20 minutes

First, prepare the sauce. Finely chop the shallot and sweat until soft in the olive oil. Flake the crabmeat and remove any cartilage. Chop the parsley leaves and add them and the crab to the pan. Cook over high heat for 1 minute, then add the vodka and tilt the pan to flame the alcohol. When the flames have died down, season well with salt and pepper.

Meanwhile, cook the spaghetti until it is *al dente*, add it to the crabmeat mixture and stir in the diced butter. Stir until the sauce has absorbed the pasta and melted the butter. Toss the pasta two or three times and serve immediately.

Seafood risotto (left, opposite); potato gnocchi with shrimp (below, left); Russian-style spaghetti with crab and vodka (below, right)

Little Fish Gnocchi

Gnocchetti di pesce

To serve 8

1 small onion

olive oil

1 garlic clove

1 bay leaf

1¼lb cod fillets

¼ cup dry white wine

1 small bunch fresh parsley

grated nutmeg

For the sauce:

1 shallot, finely chopped

olive oil

fresh sage leaves

fresh rosemary leaves

1 anchovy fillet

1½ cups tomato passata or pureed tomatoes

1 cup whipping cream

For the gnocchi:

2lb potatoes

2 cups flour, plus extra for dusting

salt

2 eggs

Preparation and cooking time: about 1 hour 10 minutes

Finely chop the onion and soften in a skillet with 3 tablespoons of olive oil, the whole garlic clove and 1 bay leaf. Cut the fish into pieces and add them to the pan. Pour in the wine, season and cook over high heat until tender and the fish flakes.

For the gnocchi, cook the potatoes in salted water for about 20 minutes or until tender. Peel and push through a potato ricer or a strainer onto a lightly floured work surface.

Remove the garlic clove and bay leaf from the pan of fish, then break up the fish with a fork and add it to the potatoes, together with the finely chopped parsley.

Season with salt, pepper and a grating of nutmeg. Add the flour and eggs, and mix to a smooth dough.

Divide the dough into several pieces and roll them along the work surface into long cylinders. Cut each cylinder into short pieces and press them against

the back of a fork to create ridges. Cook them, a few at a time, in boiling salted water until they rise to the surface. Remove with a slotted spoon and keep warm while you cook the rest.

To make the sauce, soften the finely chopped shallot in olive oil, adding a few sage and rosemary leaves and the anchovy fillet. Stir in the tomato passata and thicken the sauce with the cream. Simmer, then pour the prepared sauce over the gnocchi.

Mussel Stew with Rice

Zuppetta di cozze al riso

To serve 4

1¼ cups long-grain rice

1 small bunch fresh parsley

olive oil

½ garlic clove

about 1¾lb mussels

2¼ cups chopped tomatoes

1 medium onion, chopped

oregano

¼ cup dry white wine

Preparation and cooking time: about 40 minutes

Preheat the oven to 400°F. Cook the rice until it is *al dente* and drain well, then place in a bowl. Rinse, drain and finely chop the parsley leaves. Season the rice with a trickle of olive oil, the chopped parsley and garlic.

Thoroughly rinse the mussels and scrub them to remove the beards and any impurities. Discard any that are open. Using a sharp knife, open them, but leave the mollusc in place and the two halves of the shell still joined. Place a spoonful of the prepared rice in each shell, close and tie with kitchen string so the mussels do not open during cooking.

In a baking dish, make a bed of chopped tomatoes. Scatter the chopped onion over with a pinch each of salt and oregano. Arrange the mussels neatly on this bed, sprinkle the white wine over and a trickle of olive oil. Cook in the preheated oven for about 20 minutes. Serve the mussels piping hot, either straight from the baking dish or in a serving bowl.

Linguine with Squid Sauce

Linguine al sugo di seppia

To serve 4

2 squid, gutted

1 medium onion

1 garlic clove

olive oil

¼ cup dry white wine

1 cup chopped fresh tomatoes

12oz linguine

finely chopped fresh parsley

Preparation and cooking time: about 40 minutes

Clean the squid and remove the eyes and cartilages. Carefully take off the ink sacs, taking care not to tear them, and set aside. Rinse the squid, cut off the tentacles and cut the bodies into very thin slivers.

Peel the onion and chop it finely. Halve the garlic clove and lightly crush it, using the flat edge of a knife. Soften it and the onion in 4 tablespoons olive oil. Remove the garlic before it starts to color, and put in the squid. Cook until lightly colored, then season with salt and pepper. Add the wine, cover the pan and cook the fish for about 25 minutes. Halfway through the cooking time, thin the sauce with a ladleful of boiling water.

Five minutes before the end of cooking, add the squid ink and chopped tomatoes. Remove the lid and finish cooking, uncovered.

Meanwhile, cook the linguine until it is *al dente*. Drain the pasta, tip it into the pan and mix it with the squid sauce. Sprinkle with chopped parsley and serve.

Linguine with squid sauce (left); seafood pasta twists (right)

Seafood Pasta Twists

Fusilli "Marechiaro"

To serve 6

1¼lb firm, ripe tomatoes

1 medium onion

1 garlic clove

1 small green bell pepper

olive oil

¼ lb canned mussels

6 fresh basil leaves

a little sugar

1¼ lb pasta twists (fusilli)

1 sprig fresh parsley

Preparation and cooking time: about 1 hour

Remove the stalks from the tomatoes, wash, dry and coarsely chop them and put them through the finest disk of a food processor or purée them in a blender. Chop the onion finely with the garlic and bell pepper and sauté the mixture gently in ¼ cup of olive oil, taking care not to let it brown. Add the drained mussels, giving them a few moments to absorb the flavors, then add the tomatoes and the torn-up basil leaves. Salt cautiously, then add the pepper and a good pinch of sugar. Stir and simmer for 30 minutes over a moderate heat with the lid half on.

Meanwhile, take a large pan and bring a gallon of water to the boil. Add salt and, after a moment, plunge in the pasta and cook until just *al dente*. Drain, and add the prepared sauce plus 3 tablespoons of olive oil and a little more pepper. Stir carefully, turn into a heated tureen, sprinkle with chopped parsley and serve.

MAIN COURSES

The heart of the meal, in Italy as elsewhere in Europe, is the main course, and when it comes to fish or seafood main dishes, Italy is particularly fortunate – it is a country where you are never very far from the sea. The variety is endless, as the pages that follow demonstrate: enjoy mussels, squid and shrimp, as well as swordfish, hake or cod and sea bass – and a whole lot more as well.

Golden Jumbo Shrimp
Gamberoni Dorati

To serve 4

12 fresh jumbo shrimp

1 small leek

1 small stalk celery

1 small carrot

1 garlic clove

a few sprigs fresh parsley

4 tbsp dry white wine

flour

1 large egg

breadcrumbs

oil for frying

1 bay leaf

1 lemon

Preparation and cooking time: about 40 minutes plus 1 hour's marination

Peel the shrimp and lay them in a shallow bowl. Finely slice the leek, celery and carrot and arrange on top of the shrimp. Coarsely chop the garlic, removing the green shoot if necessary, with the parsley and add these to the shrimp. Pour over the wine and lightly sprinkle with salt. Cover the dish with plastic wrap and leave to marinate for 1 hour in a cool place or the least cold part of the refrigerator.

Remove the shrimp from the marinade, shaking off the other ingredients without wiping them, then dip them first in the flour, next in the beaten egg and finally in the breadcrumbs. Ensure that the shrimp are coated all over with these ingredients. Heat the oil with a bay leaf in a skillet, and when it is hot, pour in the shrimp and fry until they are golden brown all over. Use 2 forks to turn them over carefully while cooking.

Drain the shrimp from the oil and lay them on a plate covered with a double layer of paper towels to absorb any excess oil. Then arrange on a serving dish, sprinkle lightly with salt and garnish with slices of lemon.

Golden jumbo shrimp

Mixed Shellfish
"Capriccio" Marino

To serve 4

12 scallops

½lb shrimp

1-1¼lb mussels

5 tbsp olive oil

3 garlic cloves

a little lemon juice

1 small onion

a small bunch of parsley

5 tsp butter

¼ cup brandy

⅜ cup dry white wine

½ bouillon cube

Worcestershire sauce

Preparation and cooking time: about 45 minutes

Open the scallops using an oyster knife and remove the molluscs from their shells. Carefully separate the membranes which surround the fish and rinse the molluscs under running water to remove any sand.

Carefully peel the shrimp. Scrub the mussel shells and rinse under running water. Place the mussels in a skillet with 2 tablespoons of olive oil, 2 cloves of garlic and a few drops of lemon juice. Cover the skillet and heat briskly to open the shells. Remove the molluscs from their shells and place on a plate. Strain the cooking juices.

Finely chop the onion, a garlic clove and a small handful of parsley and fry gently in the butter and 3 tablespoons of olive oil. Add the scallops, shrimp and mussels and cook for a few minutes. Pour over the brandy and dry white wine. Season with the crumbled half bouillon cube and a generous dash of Worcestershire sauce. Add 3-4 tablespoons of the strained mussel cooking juices and simmer until a light sauce has formed. Stir in a little chopped parsley and serve.

Gray Mullet with Shellfish

Cefali con Crema di Molluschi

To serve 4

¾lb mussels

½lb clams

4 grey mullet, together weighing about 2lb

2 garlic cloves

a handful of parsley

1 bay leaf

olive oil

1 small onion

⅔ cup sparkling white wine

a pinch of cornstarch

¼ bouillon cube

breadcrumbs

1 sprig rosemary

Preparation and cooking time: about 1 hour plus 1 hour's soaking

Scrape the mussel shells clean with a knife and then leave to soak in cold water for about 1 hour, together with the clams. Cut off the fins and clean the mullet. Rinse and dry thoroughly.

Place the mussels and clams in a skillet with 2 lightly crushed garlic cloves, a few sprigs of parsley and a small bay leaf. Pour in 2 tablespoons of olive oil, cover the pan and heat gently to open the shells. Remove from the heat and leave to cool. Remove the molluscs from their shells and strain the juices.

Finely chop the onion and a small handful of parsley and fry gently in 4 tablespoons of olive oil. Add the molluscs and cook for a few minutes. Pour over half the sparkling wine and 4-5 tablespoons of the strained juices in which the cornstarch has been dissolved. Season with the crumbled quarter bouillon cube and simmer for a few minutes. Place in the blender and blend vigorously. Pour back into the pan and keep hot.

Coat the mullet in breadcrumbs. Heat 5 tablespoons of olive oil and a sprig of rosemary in a skillet and fry the mullet until golden brown on both sides. Sprinkle with salt and pepper and pour over the remaining sparkling wine. Allow the wine to evaporate and then transfer the fish to a warmed dish. Top with the creamed shellfish and garnish as desired.

Mixed shellfish

Taranto Style Mussels
Cozze Tarantine

To serve 4

1-1¼lb tomatoes

2½ lb fresh mussels

1 garlic clove

plenty of olive oil

¾ lb potatoes

½ lb zucchini

¾ lb onion

2 tbsp grated Pecorino cheese

1 sprig fresh parsley

Preparation and cooking time: about 1¾ hours

Parboil the tomatoes and then peel and slice them thinly, discarding the seeds. Scrape and rinse the mussels and place them in a skillet with the sliced garlic clove and 2 tablespoons of olive oil. Cover the pan and heat briskly to open the shells. Discard the empty half of each shell and place the half containing the mollusc on a plate. Strain the cooking juices into a bowl.
Peel and wash the potatoes and slice them, not too thinly. Top and tail the zucchini and cut them into slices about ⅛ inch thick. Slice the onion very finely.
Preheat the oven to 325°F. Grease a large ovenproof pan or dish with plenty of olive oil and line the bottom of it with a quarter of the onion rings. Arrange all the potato slices on top in one layer. Add another layer of onion rings and sprinkle with salt. Arrange half the mussels on top of the onion rings. Add half the tomatoes and season with pepper and a tablespoon of grated Pecorino cheese. Add another layer of onion rings, then all the zucchini slices and then the rest of the onion. Sprinkle with salt. Add another layer of mussels and top with the remaining tomato and a little pepper.
Sprinkle with another tablespoon of grated Pecorino cheese and pour on all the strained mussel juices and 5-6 tablespoons of oil. Add a few young leaves of parsley and cover the pan with a lid or with aluminum foil. Bake in the oven for about 1 hour or until the potatoes and zucchini are tender. Serve.

Octopus with Tomatoes and Olives
Moscardini, Pomodori e Olive

To serve 4-6

2¼lb fresh small octopuses

1 tender rib celery

1 small onion

1 sprig fresh parsley

2 small garlic cloves

¼ cup olive oil

1-1¼lb tomatoes

1 piece lemon rind

8 green olives in brine, pitted

celery leaves for garnish

Preparation and cooking time: about 2½ hours

Remove the "beak", eyes and viscera from the octopuses' body pouches and discard them. Wash and drain the octopuses. Trim the celery rib and chop it finely with the onion, parsley and garlic. Heat the olive oil in a saucepan and lightly fry the chopped vegetables. Trim, wash and chop the tomatoes and process them in a blender. Add them to the pan, stir the mixture and bring it slowly to the boil.
Beat the octopus tentacles with a wooden meat mallet and stir them into the boiling sauce. Add a piece of lemon rind. Season with a little salt and pepper and bring the mixture back to the boil. Lower the heat, cover the pan and cook for about 1¾ hours, stirring occasionally. If the sauce reduces too much, pour on a little boiling water.
Stir in the olives and cook for 15 minutes more. Test and adjust the seasoning according to taste. Serve topped with a few finely chopped celery leaves.

Stuffed Bream
Pagellini alla Ghiotta

To serve 4

8 small fresh bream

1-2 sprigs fresh parsley

2-3 leaves fresh basil

2 tbsp capers

2 anchovy fillets in oil

a little oregano

7 tbsp fresh white breadcrumbs

1 egg

1 egg, hard-boiled

olive oil

⅓ cup dry white wine

Preparation and cooking time: about 1¼ hours

Cut the fins off and scale and clean the fish. Rinse under running water and dry thoroughly. Finely chop 1 sprig of the parsley, the basil, the capers and the drained anchovy fillets. Stir in a little oregano and 4 tablespoons of breadcrumbs and bind the mixture with a beaten egg. Season with salt and pepper. Stuff the bream with the prepared mixture and sew up with kitchen twine.
Preheat the oven to 375°F. Mix the remaining breadcrumbs with the crumbled yolk of the hard-boiled egg and a tablespoon of olive oil. Arrange the bream in a well-greased ovenproof serving dish. Brush them with olive oil and sprinkle with a little salt. Top with the bread and egg mixture and a little finely chopped parsley. Sprinkle with olive oil and cook in the oven for 25-30 minutes. Pour on the white wine and cover with foil. Return to the oven for about 10 minutes to finish cooking and serve immediately.

Octopus with tomatoes and olives and Taranto style mussels

Red Mullet and Hake with Anchovies

Triglie e Merluzzetti all'Acciuga

To serve 5

5 red mullet, together weighing ¾lb

5 baby hake, together weighing ¾lb

4-5 tbsp olive oil

1 garlic clove

1 sprig parsley

2 anchovy fillets

2 tbsp breadcrumbs

oregano

1 tbsp lemon juice

1 lemon, sliced

a little dry white wine

Preparation and cooking time: about 45 minutes

Scale and de-fin the mullet. Gut the hake and mullet and rinse well under running water and dry.

Oil an ovenproof dish which is large enough to hold all the fish without any overlap. Preheat the oven to 375°F.

Finely chop a large garlic clove, a sprig of parsley and 2 well-drained anchovy fillets and place them in a shallow bowl. Add 2 tablespoons of breadcrumbs, a little oregano and a generous pinch of salt and pepper. Mix.

In another shallow bowl, beat a tablespoon of lemon juice with 3 tablespoons of olive oil and a large pinch of salt to form a smooth sauce. Dip the fish one by one in the sauce and then sprinkle them with the breadcrumb mixture. Arrange on the ovenproof dish, alternating the 2 different types of fish.

Place half-slices of lemon between the heads of the fish and sprinkle with a little olive oil. Cook in the oven for about 15 minutes, pouring on a little white wine halfway through cooking. Serve.

Fried Mixed Seafood

Frittura "Misto Mare"

To serve 4

⅔ cup mayonnaise

juice of ½ lemon

Worcestershire sauce

1 tsp mustard

paprika

1 sprig parsley, finely chopped

2 gherkins, finely chopped

1 tbsp capers, finely chopped

oil for frying

¾lb mixed seafood

½lb squid rings

Preparation and cooking time: about 30 minutes

Mix the mayonnaise and lemon juice and season with a splash of Worcestershire sauce, the mustard and a pinch of paprika. Add the chopped parsley, gherkins and capers to the mayonnaise. Blend to a smooth sauce. Check and adjust seasoning to taste. Pour into a serving bowl or jug.

Heat plenty of oil in a skillet and fry the mixed seafood and squid briskly until crisp and golden (2-3 minutes should be enough). Drain well on paper towels and arrange on a warm plate. Garnish and serve with the prepared sauce.

Red mullet and hake with anchovies

Bream San Marco

Orata "San Marco"

To serve 6

1 gilt-head bream, weighing about 3¼lb

1 small onion, thinly sliced

1 small carrot, thinly sliced

1 small stalk celery, thinly sliced

3 tbsp butter

1 garlic clove

1 small bay leaf

½ cup dry white wine

½ cup fish stock

2-3 whole black peppercorns

olive oil

a handful of fresh parsley

3 anchovy fillets in oil

Worcestershire sauce

1 tbsp mustard

juice of ½ lemon

Preparation and cooking time: about 1 hour

Prepare the fish: Remove the fins, scale carefully and gut. Rinse and dry. Sauté the onion, carrot and celery in 1 tablespoon of the butter. Add the lightly crushed garlic clove and the bay leaf and pour on the white wine and fish stock. Add the whole peppercorns, half-cover the pan and simmer gently until almost all the liquid has been absorbed.

Preheat the oven to 400°F. Arrange half the vegetables on a large sheet of buttered aluminum foil. Lay the fish on top and cover with the remaining vegetables. Season with a pinch of salt and a little olive oil. Wrap the foil around the fish, place on a baking pan and cook in the oven for about 30 minutes.

Meanwhile, finely chop a handful of parsley and the anchovy fillets and place them in a bowl. Add a generous dash of Worcestershire sauce, the mustard, lemon juice and 4 tablespoons of olive oil. Mix carefully, test and adjust the seasoning to taste.

Take the fish from the oven, unwrap it and cut off the head and tail. Discard the vegetables. Divide the fish in half and remove all the bones. Arrange the two fillets on a warmed dish, cover with the prepared sauce, garnish and serve while still hot.

Hake in Velvety Sauce with Herbs

Naselli Supremi

To serve 6

3 very fresh hake, each weighting ¾-1lb

1 medium onion

1 stick celery

3 garlic cloves

2 bay leaves

fresh parsley

6 black peppercorns

1 cup dry white wine

flour

½ cup vegetable oil

2 fresh basil leaves

1 sprig fresh tarragon

6 tbsp butter

½ cup fresh whipping cream

Preparation and cooking time: about 2 hours

Remove the fins from the fish and clean them. Wash and dry the fish, cut off their heads, remove all the bones, and skin the fillets. Put the heads, bones, and skin in a small saucepan with the halved onion, the chopped celery, 2 crushed garlic cloves, 2 bay leaves, 4-5 parsley sprigs, and 6 black peppercorns, the white wine, and 2½ cups of cold water, salt lightly and bring slowly to the boil. Skim the liquid and simmer it, uncovered, for about 15 minutes. Strain it through a fine sieve.

Roll the 6 fillets of hake in the flour and shake off the excess, then fry them gently in the heated vegetable oil and 1 lightly crushed garlic clove. When they are cooked and lightly browned, remove the fillets and drain them on paper towels. Preheat the oven to 400°F.

Finely chop a handful of parsley with 2 basil leaves and the leaves of a sprig of tarragon. In a small saucepan melt 4 tablespoons of the butter, and mix in ⅓ cup of flour; pour on to this *roux* 2½ cups of the prepared fish stock, pouring it in a trickle, stirring constantly to obtain a smooth sauce. Bring to the boil stirring all the time; remove from the heat, mix in the cream and the chopped herbs, taste and, if necessary, adjust the seasoning.

Pour a third of the sauce into an ovenproof pan large enough to contain the fish fillets, arrange them in the dish and cover them with the remaining sauce, then sprinkle with the rest of the butter, melted in a *bain-marie*. Place the pan in the oven for about 15 minutes, then serve.

Lenten pie

Lenten Pie

Sfogliata di Magro

To serve 6-8

¾ lb puff pastry

1 medium onion

1 large garlic clove

a little parsley

4 tbsp olive oil

¾lb frozen squid (rings and tentacles)

3 tbsp dry white wine

½lb peeled tomatoes

1¾ cups frozen peas

about ¼ cup butter

2½ tbsp flour

½ cup milk

nutmeg

2 eggs

breadcrumbs

Preparation and cooking time: 1¾ hours plus any thawing time

Defrost the pastry if using frozen. Slice the onions, chop a large garlic clove and a small bunch of parsley and soften them in the oil. Then add the frozen squid, lower the heat to simmer, cover the pan and allow to thaw, stirring from time to time. Now add the wine, put the tomatoes through a food processor and add these, with the frozen peas. Add a little salt and pepper, stir, then cook in a covered pan over a moderate heat for about 30 minutes, when the squid and the peas should be quite tender and the liquid thickened. Preheat the oven to 400°F.

While the squid and pea mixture is cooling, prepare a thick Béchamel sauce. Melt 2 tablespoons of butter in a pan, add the flour and cook for a minute or two; pour in the boiling milk, add salt and nutmeg and cook gently for a few minutes. Add the sauce to the squid and peas, then the beaten eggs and a little salt.

Line a buttered 9-inch round pie dish with the puff pastry. Prick the base and sprinkle with a heaping tablespoon of breadcrumbs, then pour in the prepared mixture and bake for about 30 minutes.

Fried Sardines with Cheese

Sarde al Formaggio, Fritte

To serve 4

16 large fresh sardines

⅜ cup cold milk

2½ cups fresh breadcrumbs

½ cup grated Parmesan cheese

oil for frying

1 bay leaf

1 large garlic clove

Preparation and cooking time: about 1 hour

Lighly scale then gut the sardines. Wash quickly under running water and dry. Slit right down to the tail and remove the backbone and all the small bones, but leave on the head and the tail. Sprinkle with salt and pepper and dip them in the milk. Mix the breadcrumbs and grated Parmesan cheese and thoroughly coat the sardines in this mixture. Lay the sardines on a large tray.

Heat oil in a large skillet and add a bay leaf and the crushed garlic. When the garlic has browned and the oil is very hot, remove the garlic and bay leaf and put in the sardines, a few at a time. Fry until they are golden brown, turning them with a spatula. Remove them from the pan and drain them on a dish covered with a double thickness of paper towels, then arrange them on a preheated serving dish. Keep them warm while you cook the others. Garnish as you please. Serve immediately.

Swordfish Rolls

Involtini di Pesce Spada

To serve 4

1 small onion

olive oil

8 thin slices swordfish, weighing about ½lb, and a further ¼lb swordfish scraps

2 fresh basil leaves

1 tbsp chopped parsley

⅔ cup breadcrumbs

2oz Provolone cheese, finely diced

1 egg

juice of ½ lemon

oregano

Preparation and cooking time: about 1 hour

Finely slice the onions and fry gently in 3 tablespoons of olive oil until transparent. Add the finely chopped swordfish scraps and cook until slightly browned. Add the chopped basil and parsley. Stir and cook for a few minutes and then add the breadcrumbs. Cook for a little longer and then mash to a paste.

Add the Provolone cheese, the egg and a little salt and pepper and mix thoroughly. Adjust the seasoning to taste. Leave to cool.

Lightly beat the slices of swordfish with a meat mallet and spread the prepared mixture on them. Roll them up and secure the rolls with kitchen twine or wooden toothpicks. Preheat the broiler. Brush the rolls with olive oil and broil them, turning occasionally to ensure that they cook evenly.

Pour 6 tablespoons of olive oil into a bowl and, stirring with a fork or whisk, blend in 3 tablespoons of boiling water, the juice of half a lemon, a pinch of oregano, and a little salt and pepper. Arrange the swordfish rolls on a warmed dish and serve with the prepared sauce.

Fried sardines with cheese

Scallops au Gratin
Capesante Gratinate

To serve 4

a few sprigs parsley

2 small garlic cloves

16 scallops

4 tbsp butter

olive oil

fresh white breadcrumbs

⅜ cup dry white wine

16 green olives in brine

2 tbsp flour

⅔ cup fish stock

⅓ cup fresh cream

1 egg yolk

2 tbsp Emmental cheese

Preparation and cooking time: about 1¼ hours

Chop the parsley and garlic finely. Wash the scallops and heat them gently in a skillet until the shells open. Remove the molluscs and discard the grayish flesh and the little black sac which is attached to each. Rinse and drain carefully. Scrub the shells clean under running water, dry and reserve.

Heat 2 tablespoons of the butter and 2 tablespoons of oil in an ovenproof dish and fry the chopped parsley and garlic for a few minutes. Coat the scallops in the breadcrumbs, put them in the pan and fry them briskly until golden on both sides. Sprinkle with the wine and season with salt and pepper to taste.

While the wine is evaporating, prepare the sauce by heating the remaining butter in a separate saucepan. Stir in the flour, then add the fish stock and cream. Cook gently for a few minutes. Remove the sauce from the heat and add the egg yolk. Preheat the oven to 425°F.

Once the wine has reduced by at least two thirds, return the scallops to their shells, pour the juice from the pan over them and put a sliced, pitted olive on the top of each one. Cover the scallops with the sauce and sprinkle with the Emmental cheese. Place in the oven for 4-5 minutes. Serve immediately.

Squid in Rhine Wine
Calamaretti in Carpione, alla Renana

To serve 4

1lb cleaned squid

flour

frying oil

1 large onion

olive oil

2 garlic cloves

1 bay leaf

4 whole black peppercorns

3 tbsp white wine vinegar

1⅓ cups white German wine

1 bouillon cube

Worcestershire sauce

Preparation and cooking time: about 1 hour plus 12 hours' refrigeration

Rinse the squid and drain them well, then flour them and fry a few at a time in very hot oil. When crisp and golden, lift them out with a slotted spoon and drain them on paper towels.

Slice the onion very finely and sauté it in 5 tablespoons of olive oil with 2 whole garlic cloves; discard the garlic when it is brown. Add the bay leaf and peppercorns and, after a few moments, the vinegar, the wine, the crumbled bouillon cube and a dash of Worcestershire sauce. Allow to simmer, uncovered, over a moderate heat until the liquid has been reduced to about one third. Discard the peppercorns.

Place the fried squid in a deep dish and pour the liquid, with the onion, over them. Leave to cool at room temperature, then cover the dish with plastic wrap and keep in a cool place (or the least cold part of the refrigerator) for at least 12 hours before serving, carefully turning the squid over after 6 hours.

Monkfish with an Aromatic Sauce

Pescatrice in Salsa Aromatica

To serve 6

1 small onion

1 small stalk celery

1 small carrot

2 tbsp butter

3 tbsp olive oil

2 garlic cloves

2 bay leaves

¼ lb shrimp, unpeeled

1⅛ cups dry white wine

1 tsp tomato paste

1 tsp cornstarch

½ bouillon cube

1 monkfish weighing about 1¾ lb, head removed

1 sprig rosemary

2 or 3 sage leaves

Worcestershire sauce

celery leaves for garnish

Preparation and cooking time: about 1¼ hours

Preheat the oven to 400°F. Finely slice the onion, celery and carrot. Heat in a saucepan with the butter and 2 tablespoons of olive oil. Add a lightly crushed garlic clove and a small bay leaf. Fry gently but do not brown. Then put in the shrimp and sauté for a few minutes. Pour in half the wine and simmer until the wine has almost evaporated. Dissolve the tomato paste and the cornstarch in about ⅝ cup of cold water, pour into the pan and stir. Crumble in the bouillon cube and simmer until the liquid has reduced by half.

Remove the bay leaf and blend the mixture at maximum speed for a couple of minutes. Filter the mixture through a fine strainer, taste and add salt if required. Keep the sauce hot over a double boiler.

Clean the fish and remove the dorsal and ventral fins, then brush all over with olive oil, sprinkle with salt and place in a dish large enough to hold the whole fish. Surround with a sprig of rosemary, sage leaves, a garlic clove and a small bay leaf. Put in the oven for about 30 minutes, moistening from time to time with the remaining white wine.

Towards the end of the cooking, add a dash of Worcestershire sauce. Place the fish on a preheated serving dish and pour over some of the sauce. Serve the rest in a sauceboat. Sprinkle chopped celery leaves over the fish for garnish.

Marine Style Clams

Cappe Chione alla Marinara

To serve 6

24 fresh clams

1 bay leaf

8 white peppercorns

2-3 sprigs fresh parsley

1 small onion

1 garlic clove

3 tbsp olive oil

2 egg yolks

5 tbsp whipping cream

Preparation and cooking time: about 40 minutes plus at least 2 hours' soaking

Soak the clams in plenty of lightly salted cold water for a long time, frequently turning them and changing the water at least twice. Finally wash them well, one by one, under running water, placing them in a saucepan as they are done.

Cover them with cold water and add the bay leaf, peppercorns and almost all the parsley. Bring gradually to the boil, keeping the lid on but stirring from time to time. Take them off the heat, lift them out, rinse again in the cooking water if there is any trace of sand and keep them covered in a large deep serving dish.

Chop the onion and garlic finely and fry them gently in the oil, taking care not to brown them. Pour in the white wine and half a glass of the clams' cooking water strained through a cloth. Simmer for 5 or 6 minutes then thicken with the egg yolks beaten together with the cream. Taste the sauce (which will be fairly runny), adjust the seasoning, pour it over the clams, sprinkle with chopped parsley and serve at once.

It is essential that all the sand is removed from the clams and that they should not be overcooked – being somewhat leathery, they would then become inedible.

Monkfish in an aromatic sauce (top left); *marine style clams* (left)

Cheesy Fishcakes with Parsley Sauce

Polpette di Pesce

To serve 6

1 dry bread roll

4-5 sprigs fresh parsley

2 garlic cloves

¼ lb Provolone cheese

1¼lb filleted fish (whiting, swordfish, hake)

1 small lemon

2 eggs

breadcrumbs

flour

oil for frying

2 tbsp butter

1 cup fish stock

Preparation and cooking time: about 45 minutes

Soften the bread in warm water. Wash the parsley, reserving 2 tablespoons of it, and chop it finely with a garlic clove. Grate the cheese. Chop the fish coarsely, making sure it contains no bones or bits of skin. Grate the lemon rind. Squeeze the bread well to get rid of the water and put all these ingredients together in a bowl with the 2 eggs. Season with freshly ground pepper and salt to taste.

Mix the ingredients thoroughly and add sufficient breadcrumbs to make a mixture that can be made into 12 sausage shapes with your hands. Roll them separately in the flour, coating them evenly but not too thickly. Heat a large skillet with plenty of oil, then fry the fishcakes gently, turning them frequently so that they are cooked through and nicely browned on all sides. When they are done, lift them from the pan with a slotted spatula, drain them for a moment on paper towels, arrange them on a serving dish and keep them warm.

Crush a garlic clove and brown it in the butter in a small pan. Discard the garlic and add 2 tablespoons of flour to the butter, mixing until smooth with a wooden spoon or a small whisk. Gradually add the boiling fish stock and

bring to the boil, stirring continuously. Remove from the heat, flavor with a teaspoon of the lemon juice and add 2 tablespoons of chopped parsley. Use this sauce to coat the 12 fishcakes and serve them at once, garnished to taste.

Carp Poached in Court-Bouillon

Carpa in Court-Bouillon

To serve 6

1 large onion

1 celery heart

1 carrot

1 small lemon

3 cloves

1 bay leaf

5-6 whole black peppercorns

2¼ cups dry white wine

1 rainbow carp, weighing 4lb

⅝ cup butter

Preparation and cooking time: about 1¾ hours

Clean and slice the onion, celery, carrot and lemon. Place them in a pan with the cloves, bay leaf, peppercorns, the wine and 10 pints of water. Salt sparingly and boil over a moderate heat for about 1 hour. Strain the liquid into a fish kettle and leave it to become tepid.

Clean the carp carefully, rinse and drain it and put it in the now cool court-bouillon. Return to the heat and cook for about 30 minutes from the time it comes to the boil. It should simmer very gently, otherwise the fish will break up. Remove the fish kettle from the heat but leave the fish in the broth for another 10 minutes or so. Clarify the butter in a small pan (warm it gently until floating impurities can be skimmed off and others sink to the bottom); pour off the clear part and keep it warm in a *bain-marie*.

Meanwhile, lift out the carp, drain it well, carefully remove the skin and arrange it on a suitable dish. Serve at once accompanied by the butter in a warm sauceboat.

Deep-fried Dogfish with Egg Sauce

Palombo in Frittura con Salsa d'Uova

To serve 4

2 eggs, hard-boiled

1 baby onion

1 large sprig fresh parsley

juice of 1 lemon

½ cup olive oil

oil for frying

¾-1lb dogfish fillets in batter

Preparation and cooking time: about 30 minutes

Mash the hard-boiled egg yolks. Finely chop the baby onion and the parsley and add to the egg yolks. Season with a pinch of salt and pepper and stir in the lemon juice a little at a time. Gradually pour in the olive oil, stirring constantly. Bind the sauce with 2 teaspoons of water and pour into a sauceboat.

Heat plenty of oil in a large skillet and fry the dogfish fillets until golden brown. Drain on paper towels. Arrange on a dish and serve immediately with the egg sauce.

Carp poached in court-bouillon and cheesy fishcakes with parsley sauce

Swordfish Skewers
Spiedini di Pesce Spada

To serve 4

1 red and 1 yellow bell pepper, each weighing about ¾ lb

2 thick slices of swordfish, together weighing 1¼lb

flour

olive oil

1 garlic clove

½ cup dry white wine

Worcestershire sauce

Preparation and cooking time: about 1 hour

Broil the peppers, turning them often, to scorch the skins. Wrap them individually in paper towels and set them aside for a few minutes. Peel, cut them in half, remove the seeds and stem, then cut them into 1½-inch squares.

Remove the skin from the swordfish and cut each slice into 16 small pieces of similar size. Thread 8 pieces on a long wooden skewer, alternating with the pepper squares, and beginning and ending with a pepper square. Make 4 skewers. Roll each skewer in the flour, shaking off the excess. Arrange the skewers side by side in a large skillet containing 5 tablespoons of hot oil. Flavor with a slightly crushed garlic clove. Let the skewers of fish brown well, then sprinkle with the white wine and season with a generous dash of Worcestershire sauce and some salt. Let the wine evaporate almost completely and serve on a heated plate, garnished to your taste.

Hake with Tomato Sauce
Filetti di Nasello Infuocati

To serve 6

3 hake, each weighing about ¾lb

milk

flour

olive oil

½lb firm ripe tomatoes

⅔ cup fish stock

2 basil leaves

granulated sugar

1 garlic clove

½ green pepper; scorched and peeled

1 tsp cornstarch

Preparation and cooking time: about 1 hour

Dip the filleted hake first in lightly salted cold milk, then roll them in flour. Heat 5 tablespoons of olive oil in a skillet large enough to hold all the fish. When the oil is hot add the fillets and brown, adding salt and pepper to taste. As soon as they are cooked, remove the fillets from the pan and arrange them fanwise on a heatproof dish, without overlapping them. Cover with foil and keep them warm.

Chop and purée the tomatoes, then whisk them together with the fish stock. Strain the mixture through a fine sieve into the skillet used to fry the fillets. Add 2 basil leaves, a pinch of sugar, a slightly crushed garlic clove, salt, pepper, and the finely chopped sweet pepper. Simmer for about 10 minutes, then thicken the sauce with a teaspoon of cornstarch dissolved in 5 tablespoons of cold water; stir and simmer for a few more minutes. Discard the garlic and basil. Pour the sauce over the fish fillets and serve at once, garnishing as you wish.

Seafood Pilau
Pilaf Marinaro

To serve 4

½lb cod fillets

1½ bouillon cubes

1 medium onion

olive oil

¾lb rice

a little powdered saffron

1 small leek

2 garlic cloves

¼lb shrimp

dry white wine

Worcestershire sauce

a few tender celery leaves

Preparation and cooking time: about 30 minutes

Cut the cod fillets into ¾-inch cubes. Preheat the oven to 400°F. Boil 2½ cups of water with 1 bouillon cube. Finely chop the onion and sauté it in 4 tablespoons of olive oil, in an ovenproof pan. Add the rice and cook it for a few moments, color it with the saffron, stir, and immediately pour on the boiling stock. Bring back to the boil, then put the dish in the oven for about 15 minutes, until the rice has absorbed the liquid completely.

Meanwhile cut the leek into rings and finely chop the garlic. Put them both in a skillet with 3 tablespoons of olive oil and sauté them gently. Then put the cubes of cod and the prawns in the pan. Cook them over a fairly vigorous heat. Flavor with large a dash of Worcestershire sauce. Remove the rice from the oven and mix it with the seafood. Scatter over a few tender celery leaves, coarsely chopped, then serve.

Hake with tomato sauce (top) *and swordfish skewers*

Gourmet Fried Fish
Tracine del Gourmet

To serve 4

16 small weevers or star-gazers, weighing about 2lb in all

flour

4 jumbo shrimp

4 shallots

2-3 sprigs parsley

4 tbsp olive oil

½ cup dry white wine

½lb peeled tomatoes

⅜ cup fish stock

2 fresh basil leaves

½ bay leaf

oil for frying

Preparation and cooking time: about 1 hour

Remove the fins and the dangerous spines around the gills and gut the fish. Wash the fish rapidly and dry them carefully. Coat them one by one in the flour and shake off the excess. Shell the shrimp.

Chop the shallots finely with the leaves of 2-3 sprigs of parsley, then sauté very gently in 4 tablespoons of olive oil, taking care not to brown. Add the shrimp, fry them for a few moments, then moisten them with the white wine and let it evaporate by a third before putting the peeled tomatoes in the pan, after passing them through the food processor using the finest disk. Also add the fish stock, 2 leaves of basil and half a bay leaf, and salt and pepper to taste, then cook over a fairly high heat for about 15 minutes. Stir from time to time and moisten with a little boiling water if necessary.

While the shrimp mixture is cooking, heat plenty of oil in a large skillet, fry the whole fish, drain them well when tender and lay them on a plate covered with a double sheet of paper towels. Salt them and arrange them on an appropriate serving dish. Pour the shrimp mixture over them, having removed the basil and bay leaf, and serve immediately.

Rolled Sole with Peas

Involtini di sogliole ai piselli

To serve 4

¼ cup frozen peas

10 sole fillets

¼ cup whipping cream

4 tbsp butter, softened and diced

1 shallot

¼ cup dry white wine

1 small bunch fresh parsley

Preparation and cooking time: about 1 hour

Preheat the oven to 400°F. To make the stuffing, cook the peas until tender in boiling salted water, then puree two of the sole fillets and add them to the peas, season, add 4 tablespoons of cream and mix to a smooth paste. Put the mixture into a pastry bag fitted with a small plain nozzle.

Lightly beat out the remaining sole fillets, salt them and roll up each one around a wide cork. Carefully remove the corks, then fill the cavities with the pea mixture. Grease a baking dish with all the butter and arrange the filled sole rolls in the dish.

Finely chop the shallot and scatter it over the sole rolls, then add the remaining cream, the wine and some finely chopped parsley. Cover the dish with foil and cook in the preheated oven for 20 minutes.

Transfer the rolls to a serving dish and, if you wish, garnish with cooked, sliced zucchini. Serve at once.

Baked Stuffed Sea Bass
Spigola Farcita, al Forno

To serve 8

1 small onion

2 garlic cloves

a few sprigs parsley

5 tbsp olive oil

¼lb cod fillet

1 slice white bread soaked in milk

1 egg

10 shrimp

15 mussels

breadcrumbs

1 sea bass, weighing about 2¾ lb

2-3 bay leaves

3-4 tbsp dry white wine

Preparation and cooking time: about 1½ hours

Chop the onion, 1 garlic clove and the parsley and sauté in 3 tablespoons of oil. Leave to cool. Cut the cod fillet into small pieces, drain the milk from the bread and then place the sautéed mixture, the cod, bread, egg and a pinch of salt and pepper in the blender. Blend briskly for a couple of minutes. Shell the shrimp, dice them and add to the blended mixture.

Scrape and wash the mussel shells and place them in a skillet with a tablespoon of oil, a garlic clove and a few leaves of parsley. Cover the pan and place on a high heat to open the shells. Shell the mussels and add to the blended mixture. Strain the mussels' cooking juices through cheesecloth and reserve. If the stuffing seems too liquid, add some breadcrumbs and leave to stand in a cool place. Preheat the oven to 400°F.

Cut the fins off the bass, scale it, wash it under running water and dry it. Remove the spine, bones and entrails and clean the inside of the fish with paper towels. Stuff the bass with the prepared mixture and sew up the opening. Brush the fish with olive oil and coat it thoroughly in breadcrumbs.

Place 2 or 3 bay leaves in the bottom of a well-oiled ovenproof pan, put the fish in the pan and bake in the oven for about 30 minutes. Turn the fish once or twice during cooking, being careful not to damage it, and sprinkle it with 3-4 tablespoons each of white wine and the cooking liquid from the mussels. Serve the fish cut into large slices.

Aromatic Stewed Clams
Telline in Umido Aromatico

To serve 4

2½lb clams

a handful of fresh parsley

1 garlic clove

4 fresh basil leaves

5 tbsp olive oil

¾-1 lb firm ripe tomatoes

extra basil leaves for garnish

Preparation and cooking time: about 40 minutes plus 1 hour's soaking

Wash the clams well under cold running water then soak them in a bowl of cold salted water for about 1 hour to release any sand. Meanwhile, finely chop the parsley with the garlic, removing the green shoot first, and the basil. Put the herbs in a large skillet with the olive oil and cook over a moderate heat. Do not allow to brown.

Blanch the tomatoes in boiling water, peel and chop them. Add them to the skillet and stir with a wooden spoon. Cook for about 10 minutes then drain the clams thoroughly and put these in too. Stir, and cover the skillet for a few minutes until the clams have opened. Then remove the lid and simmer gently, stirring from time to time. After 5-6 minutes season with freshly ground pepper, taste and correct the seasoning if necessary. Serve in a warmed bowl or serving dish, garnished with fresh basil.

Sea Bream with Herbs
Pagellini alle Erbe

To serve 6

12 small sea bream

4oz canned tuna in oil

parsley

1 tbsp capers

1 garlic clove

1 tbsp breadcrumbs

1 egg

2 bay leaves

olive oil

rosemary

1 sprig each fresh chervil and marjoram

¼ cup dry white wine

Preparation and cooking time: about 1¼ hours

Wash the fish one at a time under cold running water, then dry them thoroughly both inside and out. Preheat the oven to 400°F.

Finely chop the well-drained tuna with a handful of parsley, the capers and half a garlic clove. Place the minced mixture in a small bowl, add the breadcrumbs, a little salt and a generous grinding of pepper, then bind with the egg. Fill each fish with the mixture, then sew up the openings.

Put 2 crushed bay leaves and the fish into an oiled rectangular ovenproof dish. Brush them with olive oil and season with salt, white pepper, and a small sprig of rosemary. Finely chop the chervil leaves and the marjoram and sprinkle the herbs over the fish.

Put them in the oven for about 20 minutes. Halfway through the cooking time moisten them with the wine. Serve them from the same dish.

Aromatic stewed clams (top)*; baked stuffed sea bass* (bottom)

Sea Bream with Mussel Sauce

Pagelli con Salsa di Cozze

To serve 4

¾-1 lb fresh mussels

1½ garlic cloves

olive oil

1 lemon

1 small bay leaf

1 small onion

3-4 sprigs fresh parsley

a little dry white wine

½ tsp cornstarch

Worcestershire sauce

4 sea bream, each weighing about ½lb

1 tbsp breadcrumbs

Preparation and cooking time: about 1¼ hours

Preheat the oven to 375°F. Scrape the mussel shells under cold running water using a small sharp knife. Then put the mussels in a skillet with a lightly crushed garlic clove, a trickle of olive oil, a slice of lemon cut into segments and a small bay leaf. Cover the pan and place over a high heat to open the mussels.

Once they have opened, remove the mussels from their shells and strain the juices into a bowl. Finely chop the onion with the half garlic clove and a little parsley, and fry gently in 1 tablespoon of olive oil, taking care not to let the mixture brown. Then put in the mussels and, after a few seconds, pour in a little wine. Dissolve the cornstarch in the cold juices from the mussels and add to the pan. Stir and simmer for a few seconds. Flavor with a dash of Worcestershire sauce, then remove from the heat.

Oil an ovenproof dish that is just the right size to hold the bream. Scrape the fish, wash rapidly under running water and dry. Place in the dish and sprinkle with salt and pepper. Pour over the mussel sauce and sprinkle with 1 tablespoon of breadcrumbs and chopped parsley. Pour over a trickle of olive oil and lay a sheet of aluminum foil over the dish without sealing it. Bake in the oven for about 20 minutes, then serve.

Hake with Tomato and Beans

Nasello con Pomodoro e Fagioli

To serve 4

1 large hake, weighing about 1¾ lb, fins and gills removed and gutted

5 heaping tbsp breadcrumbs

1 garlic clove

3-4 sprigs fresh parsley

a few celery leaves

1 egg

1 small onion

olive oil

1¾ cups canned white beans

1¾ cups canned tomatoes

2 large fresh basil leaves

Preparation and cooking time: about 1½ hours

Preheat the oven to 375°F. Rinse the gutted fish quickly under running water and dry. Put 4 heaping tablespoons of breadcrumbs in a bowl and chop half the garlic clove together with 2-3 sprigs of parsley and a few celery leaves. Add this mixture to the bowl and bind with the egg. Season with salt and pepper. Stuff the fish with this mixture and sew up the opening.

Finely chop the onion with the remaining half garlic clove and fry in 3 tablespoons of olive oil. Drain the beans thoroughly, rinse and add to the onions, stirring with a wooden spoon. After a few minutes, add the tomatoes, mashed finely, the basil, salt and pepper. Mix and simmer for 5-6 minutes. Place the hake in an oiled ovenproof dish and pour the tomato and bean sauce all around the fish. Brush with a little olive oil and sprinkle with salt and the remaining tablespoon of breadcrumbs. Cover the dish with a sheet of aluminum foil and cook in the oven for about 25 minutes. Remove the foil 10 minutes before the fish is cooked and baste with some of the sauce. Sprinkle the cooked fish with chopped parsley and serve.

Seafood Kebabs

Spiedini del Mare

To serve 4

16 jumbo shrimp, unpeeled

16 scallops, shelled

8 green olives in brine

16 canned baby onions in oil

very fine breadcrumbs

½ garlic clove

olive oil

3 tbsp dry white wine

Preparation and cooking time: about 1 hour

Preheat the oven to 425°F. Peel the shrimp. Remove the beards and the darker flesh from the scallops then rinse rapidly, drain and dry thoroughly. Remove the pits from the olives, dry them and cut them in half widthwise. On 8 wooden skewers alternate an onion, a shrimp, half an olive and a scallop, then another onion, followed by a shrimp, then an olive and a scallop. Roll the kebabs in the breadcrumbs, pressing lightly to coat the ingredients evenly all over.

Rub the bottom of an ovenproof dish with garlic, grease it with olive oil, then place the kebabs in it, well apart. Pour over a thin trickle of olive oil and season with salt and pepper. Cook in the oven for about 10 minutes. Splash over the wine, and cook for a couple of minutes more before serving.

Hake with tomato and beans (top), *sea bream with mussel sauce* (center) and *seafood kebabs*

Florentine-style Fillet of Perch

Filetti di Pesce Persico Fiorentina

To serve 4

2¼lb fresh young spinach

4 tbsp butter

5 tbsp olive oil

nutmeg

flour

1 cup milk

1 garlic clove

2 sage leaves

16 small or 8 large fillets of perch, weighing about 2 lb in all, divided in half lengthwise

breadcrumbs

parsley for garnish

Preparation and cooking time: about 1¼ hours

Preheat the oven to 475°F. Wash the spinach thoroughly under running water. Cook in an uncovered saucepan with only the water that remains on the leaves after washing and a little coarse cooking salt for about 10 minutes, until the leaves are tender, occasionally stirring with a wooden spoon. Drain the spinach and cool under running water. Then squeeze it dry and chop coarsely.

Heat 2 tablespoons of butter and 2 tablespoons of the olive oil in a large skillet, and as soon as the fat is hot, put in the spinach and fry lightly, seasoning with a little salt, pepper and nutmeg. Then sprinkle in the flour and heat the milk before pouring that in too. Stir and simmer for a few seconds, then transfer the contents of the pan to a heatproof dish and keep warm in the oven with the door open.

Flour the fish and shake them to remove any excess. Clean and dry the pan that was used for the spinach and melt the rest of the butter and 3 tablespoons of olive oil in it, flavoring with the lightly crushed garlic and the sage leaves. Fry the fish until golden brown and season with a little salt and pepper.

Remove from the pan and arrange on the bed of spinach. Strain the juices in the pan and pour over. Sprinkle lightly with breadcrumbs and bake for a couple of minutes. Serve garnished with parsley.

Trout in Herbed Breadcrumbs

Trote al Pangrattato Aromatico

To serve 4

4 cleaned trout

2 large sprigs fresh rosemary

1 sprig fresh parsley

1 sprig fresh sage

1 garlic clove

4 slices fresh white bread

juice of ½ lemon

a little olive oil

lemon slices for garnish

Preparation and cooking time: about 50 minutes plus thawing

Defrost the trout if frozen. Drain well and dry on paper towels. Finely chop the leaves of 1 rosemary sprig, 1 parsley sprig, 3 sage leaves and a garlic clove. Crumble the bread and reduce it to fine breadcrumbs by rubbing it between your fingers. Mix the breadcrumbs with the chopped herbs and place on a large plate or tray.

Preheat the oven to 375°F. Slice the trout lengthwise and open them out. Sprinkle the insides with a little salt and pepper. Rub with a little lemon juice and brush with a little olive oil.

Coat the fish thoroughly in the herbed breadcrumbs, place them on a lightly oiled baking pan and cook in the oven for about 20 minutes or until golden brown. Arrange the trout on a warmed dish, garnish with parsley and slices of lemon and serve.

Florentine-style fillet of perch (right); trout in herbed breadcrumbs (below)

Adriatic Salt Cod with Potatoes

Baccalà dell'Adriatico

To serve 6

2 large potatoes

1 small onion

1 garlic clove

5-6 tbsp olive oil

18oz tomatoes, peeled

½ bay leaf

a pinch of sugar

1¼lb salt cod, soaked to soften and then dried

a few fresh basil leaves

Preparation and cooking time: about 1½ hours

Preheat the oven to 375-400°F. Boil a large saucepanful of water and add a little salt when it begins to boil. Peel, wash and dry the potatoes, and cut them into horizontal slices about ⅛ inch wide. Boil them for about 3 minutes. Drain and leave to cool.

Meanwhile, finely chop the onion together with the garlic. Heat 3 tablespoons of olive oil in a small saucepan and fry the onion and garlic. Peel the tomatoes and put them through the fine disk of a food processor, and add to the saucepan. Season with salt, pepper, half a bay leaf and a pinch of sugar. Mix and simmer for about 15 minutes, leaving the pan uncovered.

Cut the cod into equal pieces. Pour 2 tablespoons of olive oil into an ovenproof earthenware dish and make layers of potatoes and cod. Pour a little tomato sauce between each layer and sprinkle with the chopped basil. Pour a trickle of olive oil over the top and bake in the oven for about 1 hour. Before serving, sprinkle with more basil, freshly ground pepper and a little olive oil.

Adriatic salt cod with potatoes (top) and fried salt cod in beer batter

Trout with Tuna Fish

Trota Tonnata

To serve 6-8

1 large trout, weighing about 3½lb

6oz canned tuna in oil

1¼ cups fresh breadcrumbs

a few sprigs parsley

3 eggs

½ cup grated Parmesan cheese

olive oil

2 sprigs rosemary

2 garlic cloves

½ cup dry white wine

Preparation and cooking time: about 1½ hours

Preheat the oven to 375°F. Remove the fins from the trout and clean it. Wash quickly under cold running water, then pat dry. Open the fish out flat and fillet it, taking care not to crush the flesh in the process.

Now prepare the stuffing: drain the tuna throroughly and mash it. Add ¾ cup of the breadcrumbs and the parsley, washed, dried and finely chopped. Bind the mixture with the eggs and the Parmesan cheese, and season with a little salt and freshly ground pepper. Stuff the trout with the mixture and sew it up. Brush the entire surface of the trout with olive oil, sprinkle with the rest of the breadcrumbs and lay on a baking tray with the rosemary and lightly crushed garlic (which should remain under the trout during cooking).

Bake for about 45 minutes, turning the trout over halfway through. Splash a little wine over from time to time. Remove the trout from the oven and leave to rest for about 5 minutes. Then place on a serving dish, garnished to taste.

White Bream with Tomatoes and Peas

Sarago "Verderosso"

To serve 4

1 white bream weighing about 2½lb

2 bay leaves

1 sprig rosemary

1 garlic clove, lightly crushed

6 tbsp butter

1 onion

1 lb peeled tomatoes

2 basil leaves

a pinch of sugar

1¾ cups frozen young peas

Preparation and cooking time: about 1¼ hours

Remove the fins from the bream and scale and gut it. Wash rapidly under running water and pat dry. Stuff the fish with a bay leaf, the rosemary, the garlic and pepper. Melt 4 tablespoons of the butter. Arrange the bream in an ovenproof dish and pour over the melted butter. Leave for about 30 minutes, turning it over a couple of times.

Meanwhile, preheat the oven to 375°F. Chop the onion and gently sauté in the remaining butter in a pan. Then put the tomatoes through a food processor using the finest disk and add these to the onions. Add the basil, sugar and a little salt. Put in the frozen peas and bring to the boil. Simmer for 20-25 minutes, keeping the pan partly covered and stirring from time to time with a wooden spoon.

Put the bream in the oven for about 25 minutes, turning it once, with great care, halfway through the cooking. After this, cover it with a sheet of aluminum foil. Finally, arrange the fish on a preheated serving dish and bring to the table accompanied by the simmering tomato and pea sauce.

Fried Salt Cod in Beer Batter

Filetti di Baccalà Fritti

To serve 4

1 cup flour

1 egg

1 tbsp olive oil

1¼ cups lager

1½lb salt cod, soaked to soften and then dried

¼ cup butter

1 garlic clove

¼ cup grated Parmesan cheese

oil for frying

1 sprig fresh parsley for garnish

Preparation and cooking time: about 1½ hours

Put the flour in a dish together with ½ teaspoon of salt. Mix and make a well in the center. Separate the egg and put the yolk in the well; reserve the white. Add 1 tablespoon of olive oil and as much lager as is required to make a smooth batter that is not too runny. Take care not to let it become lumpy. Cover the dish and set aside for 1 hour.

Cut the cod into equal pieces. Heat the butter and garlic in a skillet which is large enough to contain all the fish in a single layer. As soon as the butter has melted, put in the pieces of cod and fry over a moderate heat, turning them over carefully to allow them to absorb the flavor. Remove the skillet from the heat and sprinkle over the Parmesan. Cover and leave to cool.

Heat plenty of light frying oil in a deep pan over a low heat. Whisk the egg white until it is stiff and carefully fold it into the batter using an up-and-down movement rather than a circular one. Dip the cod fillets in the batter, one at a time, and shake off any excess so they do not drip. When the oil is hot, drop them in and fry until they are golden brown and crisp all round. Remove and shake off as much oil as possible, then lay them on a plate covered with kitchen paper to absorb any remaining oil. Arrange them on a hot serving dish, garnish with the chopped parsley and serve.

Swordfish En Papillotte

Pesce spada al cartoccio

To serve 4

3 large ripe tomatoes, peeled

1 garlic clove

1 small bunch fresh parsley

4 swordfish steaks or fillets

flour for dusting

olive oil

11oz mussels

7oz clams

¼lb shelled shrimp

2 basil leaves

1 sprig fresh thyme

1 egg white

Preparation and cooking time: about 1 hour

Fold a 20- × 28-inch piece of baking parchment in half and draw a half heart shape on one side. Cut out the parchment into a heart shape. Prepare three more paper hearts in exactly the same way.

Cut the tomatoes into small pieces. Place in a bowl with the finely chopped garlic and parsley.

Rinse the swordfish steaks or fillets and flour lightly. Heat 3 tablespoons of oil in a skillet and add the fish. Brown for 2 minutes on each side.

Scrub and rinse the mussels and rinse the clams, removing beards and sand, and discarding any that are open. Put them in a saucepan and set over high heat until they open. Discard any that do not open. Heat 2 tablespoons of oil in a skillet, put in the shrimp and herbs, then, after 2–3 minutes, add the mussels and clams with their strained juices, and the tomatoes. Cook for 5 minutes. Preheat the oven to 350°F.

Lay one parchment heart on a flat plate, and arrange a piece of fish on it.

Season and add some of the mussel and shrimp sauce. Brush the edges of the heart with egg white.

Close the heart-shaped *papillotte* and place it on a lightly oiled cookie sheet. Fill and close three more hearts in the same way. Place them on the cookie sheet and trickle a little oil over. Bake in the preheated oven until well puffed up, about 20 minutes. Transfer to warmed plates and serve immediately.

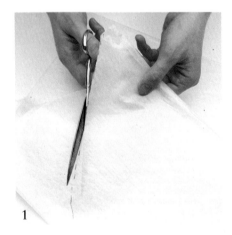

Salt Cod with Onions

Baccalà e cipolle

To serve 4

3 medium onions

olive oil

1lb salt cod, soaked overnight in cold water to soften, then drained

fresh sage leaves

milk

Preparation and cooking time: about 40 minutes

Peel the onions and slice them thickly. Sweat in a large skillet with 4 tablespoons of olive oil, stirring so the onions do not color.

Meanwhile, remove the skin and any large bones from the salt cod. Rinse the fish well and pat it dry thoroughly with paper towels, then cut it into even-sized pieces. Put the cod into the pan with the onions and cook for a few minutes over high heat. Add two or three sage leaves and season, then pour a glass of milk over. Cover the pan and cook over low heat for 25–30 minutes, turning the pieces of salt cod very carefully once or twice.

Transfer the cod to a warmed serving dish, and serve immediately.

Trout Baked in Salt

Trotelle al sale

To serve 6

6 trout, gutted and cleaned

about 4½lb coarse sea salt

fresh sage leaves

fresh parsley sprigs

To accompany: the very best-quality extra-virgin olive oil

Preparation and cooking time: about 1 hour

Preheat the oven to 400°F. Rinse the trout several times and dry with paper towels. Season the insides with salt and pepper and place a few sage leaves and a sprig of parsley in each fish.

Spread about half the salt in the bottom of a large baking dish and arrange the trout on top, laying them all on the same side. Cover the fish completely with a second layer of the remaining salt, then bake in the preheated oven for 40 minutes.

Remove the baking dish from the oven and open the salt crust (you can re-use it for a similar recipe). Remove the trout, clean off all traces of salt and remove the herbs. Arrange the fish on a serving dish, preferably warmed. Serve the trout accompanied by the best-quality extra-virgin olive oil.

Swordfish Steaks with Shrimp

Braciole di mare

To serve 4

12oz carrots

4 swordfish steaks

about 2 tbsp flour

4 tbsp butter

olive oil

⅔ cup dry red wine

¼lb uncooked shrimp

Preparation and cooking time: about 40 minutes

Trim and peel the carrots and cut them into lengths. Divide each piece vertically into four then, with a very sharp knife, trim the ends to "turn" each piece into an olive shape. Cook the carrots in plenty of boiling salted water until tender.

Dip the swordfish steaks in flour and shake off the excess. Heat half the butter with 1 tablespoon of olive oil in a skillet and put in the fish. Cook for 5–8 minutes on each side over high heat, then season, add the cooked carrots and pour the wine over. When the liquid begins to simmer, carefully take out the fish, transfer to a serving dish and keep warm. Lower the heat and boil until the wine has reduced by half.

Meanwhile, rinse and shell the shrimp. Work the remaining butter with 1 teaspoon of flour into a paste and, when the sauce has reduced enough, add the shrimp and the butter paste, stirring continuously with a wooden spoon for 3–4 minutes, until the paste has completely melted. When the sauce has become very smooth, pour it over the swordfish and serve.

Trout baked in salt (top);
swordfish steaks with shrimp (center);
salt cod with onions (right)

Baked Stuffed Trout

Trotelle ripiene, in forno

To serve 4

4 trout

butter for greasing

¼ cup dry white wine

For the stuffing:

2 whiting, white fish or salmon trout

4 tbsp whipping cream

1 small bunch fresh parsley

1 egg

1 medium red bell pepper, seeded and diced

butter

Preparation and cooking time: about 1 hour 10 minutes

Preheat the oven to 400°F. Slit the trout open from top to bottom, then, with a sharp knife, fillet the fish without removing the heads, skin or tails. Using a needle and fine white thread, sew up the two fillets of each trout following the line of the belly, and sew up a small section of the back fillets, starting from the tail end. The trout should now have a large opening along their backs. Place the prepared trout on a plate, cover with plastic wrap and chill well in the refrigerator.

Baked stuffed trout (above);
mackerel with piquant sauce (right)

To make the stuffing, puree the whiting or other fish flesh in a food processor and place in a bowl. Season, then stir in the cream, some finely chopped parsley leaves and the egg. Blend again until smooth. Sweat the pepper in a skillet with a knob of butter, then add it to the stuffing.

Take the trout out of the refrigerator and fill each one with one quarter of the stuffing. Butter a baking dish and arrange them in one layer. Pour the wine over, cover with foil and bake in the oven for about 35 minutes.

Transfer the cooked trout to a serving platter, garnish with tomato wedges and lettuce, if you wish, and serve immediately.

Mackerel with Piquant Sauce

Sgombro in salsa forte

To serve 6

---

6 whole mackerel, gutted and cleaned

---

flour for dusting

---

1 garlic clove

---

olive oil

---

10 black peppercorns, coarsely crushed

---

dry white wine

---

1 onion, finely chopped

---

1 yellow bell pepper, seeded and sliced

⅓ cup ripe olives

---

1 cup tomato passata or pureed tomatoes

Preparation and cooking time: about 30 minutes

Carefully rinse the mackerel inside and out and pat dry, then roll in flour, shaking off any excess.

Crush the garlic, using the flat edge of a knife. In a skillet, heat 4 tablespoons of oil, add the garlic and coarsely crushed peppercorns and cook for about 1 minute. Brown the mackerel on both sides, then season to taste and moisten with a very little wine, 2 or 3 tablespoons.

Remove the fish from the pan and keep warm. Add the onion and yellow bell pepper to the pan with the whole olives. Mix and sweat until the vegetables are tender, then add the tomato passata. Bring to a boil, add the mackerel again and cook over medium heat for 10 minutes.

Transfer the fish to a serving platter. Surround with the olives and spoon some of the sauce over, serving the rest separately, in a sauceboat.

Trout in Green Jackets

Trota al cartoccio verde

To serve 2

2 trout, cleaned and gutted

2 fresh dill sprigs

1 small bunch fresh parsley

10 fresh sage leaves

1 bay leaf

large green lettuce leaves

extra-virgin olive oil

Preparation and cooking time: about 50 minutes

Rinse and dry the fish, then season inside and out with salt and pepper and put a sprig of dill into each fish. Finely chop the parsley, the 10 sage leaves and the bay leaf, and scatter this mixture over the fish.

Wrap the fish in large lettuce leaves, and secure them with kitchen string. Lay the fish on the rack of a steamer, fill the bottom with simmering water and steam for about 30 minutes.

Remove the fish from the pan, untie the lettuce and place them on a serving plate. Drizzle a trickle of olive oil over and serve at once, piping hot.

Trout in green jackets (top); baby squid casserole (center); fish medallions (bottom)

Fish Vol au Vent

Sfogliatina di pesce

To serve 4

11oz frozen puff pastry dough, thawed

1 egg

¾lb turbot fillets

1 swordfish steak, about ¾lb

7oz shelled uncooked shrimp

flour for coating fish

1 shallot

olive oil

paprika

brandy

2 tomatoes, peeled and chopped

1 small bunch fresh parsley

butter for greasing

Preparation and cooking time: about 45 minutes

Preheat the oven to 400°F. Roll out the thawed dough on a lightly floured work surface into an 11- × 4-inch rectangle and a ¾-inch border of the same dimensions. Place the larger rectangle on a greased cookie sheet, brush with beaten egg, then place the border on top to make a rim. Brush again with egg, then bake in the preheated oven for about 25 minutes.

Meanwhile, to prepare the fish, thoroughly rinse the turbot, then cut into bite-sized pieces. Remove the swordfish skin and cut the flesh into bite-sized pieces. Roll the fish and the rinsed and dried shrimp in flour, shaking off any excess. Peel and finely chop the shallot, then place it in a skillet with 5 tablespoons of oil and sweat until tender. Add the prepared fish, season with salt and 1 teaspoon of paprika, and pour over a small glass of brandy (about 6 tablespoons). Tilt the pan to set light to the brandy and let it flame for a few moments, then extinguish the flame. Add the chopped tomatoes and some finely chopped parsley leaves. Lower the heat, and cook for about 6 minutes.

Reduce the oven temperature to 375°F. Take the vol au vent out of the oven and, with the point of a knife, carefully make an incision around the inside of the border, taking care not to cut right through the bottom. Push the pastry with your fingertips to make a cavity and fill this with the prepared fish mixture.

Return to the oven to heat through for 5 minutes, then serve immediately.

Baby Squid Casserole

Umido di fragolini

To serve 4

2¼lb baby squid, cleaned and gutted

olive oil

2 garlic cloves

1 tbsp capers

dried oregano

flour

¼ cup full-bodied dry red wine

1 × 14-oz can chopped tomatoes

1 small bunch fresh parsley

Preparation and cooking time: about 1 hour

Rinse the squid in cold water. Leave to drain and, in the meanwhile, heat 4 tablespoons of olive oil in a flameproof casserole. Crush the garlic, using the flat edge of a knife, and add it to the casserole, together with the chopped, drained capers and a pinch of oregano. Add the well-drained squid, cook for a few minutes, stirring with a wooden spoon, then discard the garlic. Sift 1 tablespoon of flour over the mixture, mixing it in with a wooden spoon as you do so. Pour in the wine and let it evaporate, then add the chopped tomatoes. Bring to a boil, season well and pour over a glass of boiling water.

Cover and cook over low heat for about 50 minutes. Sprinkle the dish with coarsely chopped parsley and serve piping hot.

Tuna Tart

Torta di tonno

To serve 8

heaped 3 cups flour, plus extra for dusting

1 cup plus 2 tbsp butter, softened and diced, plus extra for greasing

1 egg

For the filling:

1lb potatoes

1 slice fresh tuna, about 14oz

2 cups peeled and chopped tomatoes

1½ cups sliced zucchini

olive oil

dried oregano

1 small bunch fresh parsley

Preparation and cooking time: about 1½ hours, plus resting the dough

Pile the flour on a work surface and make a well. Put in a pinch of salt and the diced, softened butter. Incorporate the butter, then add the egg and knead the dough a little, rolling it into a ball. Wrap in plastic wrap and place in the refrigerator for 30 minutes.

Meanwhile, butter and flour a 10-inch springform cake pan. Roll out the dough on the floured surface to about ½-inch thick and use to line the springform pan, leaving enough overhanging to fold in after the pan has been filled.

Peel the potatoes. Skin the tuna and cut into bite-sized pieces.

Cover the base of the pan with about half the potatoes, then make an even layer of half the zucchini and then the chopped tomatoes.

Trickle a little olive oil over and season with pepper and a pinch of dried oregano.

Arrange the pieces of tuna on the tomatoes in a single layer. Continue to make layers of the vegetables, finishing with tomatoes. Season with salt, pepper and oregano, and moisten with about 3 tablespoons of olive oil.

Fold the overhanging dough inward, pinch up the edges and bake in the oven preheated to 400°F for about 1 hour. Take the tart out of the oven, sprinkle with finely chopped parsley leaves and serve.

Sea Bass with Zucchini
Branzino alle zucchine

To serve 8

1 large sea bass, about 4lb, cleaned and gutted

1 garlic clove

1 small bunch fresh parsley

fresh marjoram

fresh basil leaves

fresh sage leaves

fresh rosemary leaves

olive oil

¼ cup dry white wine

2 zucchini

3 slices white bread

3 tbsp grated Parmesan cheese

lemon slices and parsley sprigs for garnishing

Preparation and cooking time: about 1 hour

Preheat the oven to 350°F. Rinse the fish well, inside and out, then place it in a greased baking dish just large enough to hold it snugly.

Crush the garlic clove, using the flat edge of a knife, and chop together with the parsley and all the other fresh herbs (use these to taste). Season the inside of the fish with salt and pepper, then scatter over the chopped herb mixture. Moisten the fish with 5 tablespoons of olive oil and pour the wine over, then cook in the preheated oven for about 35 minutes.

Meanwhile, trim and rinse the zucchini, cut them into thin slices and cook for 2 minutes in a pan of boiling water. Drain and refresh under cold running water, then lay them out to dry on paper towels.

Crumb the bread in a blender and mix in the grated Parmesan. Five minutes before the fish is cooked, take the dish out of the oven and cover the bass with the sliced zucchini, arranging them like scales. Sprinkle over the bread crumb and cheese mixture, trickle over 2 tablespoons oil and return

the fish to the oven, increasing the temperature to 450°F. Cook for 5 minutes longer, or until the bread crumbs are well browned.

Take the fish out of the oven, carefully transfer it to an oval serving dish, garnish with a few slices of lemon and some parsley sprigs and serve immediately.

Steamed Whiting
Bianco di pesce al vapore

To serve 4

¼ cup dry white wine

1 shallot, peeled and halved

celery leaves

1½lb whole whitings or whitefish

1 tablespoon grated lemon peel

fresh thyme sprigs

fresh sage leaves

lettuce leaves

extra-virgin olive oil

Preparation and cooking time: about 1 hour

First prepare the cooking broth. Put about 6¼ cups water, the wine, the shallot and a few celery leaves into a fish kettle and bring to a boil.

Wash the whitings and place on the rack of the fish kettle over the by now boiling liquid. Season, then scatter on the lemon peel and a few thyme and sage leaves. Cover and steam the fish for about 30 minutes.

Take the fish kettle off the heat, place the fish on a platter and remove the skin, heads and bones. Flake the flesh, following the natural grain.

On a serving platter or individual plates, make a bed of well-rinsed and dried lettuce leaves. Arrange the flaked fish on the lettuce, season, dress with a trickle of olive oil and serve sprinkled with lemon peel, some sprigs of thyme and one or two sage leaves.

Fish medallions
Haché di mare

To serve 4

9oz monkfish tail

5oz swordfish steak

2 egg yolks

flour for dusting

olive oil

2 scallions

⅔ cup dry white wine

¼ cup tomato passata or pureed tomatoes

1 small bunch fresh parsley

fresh basil leaves

Preparation and cooking time: about 30 minutes

Remove the skin from the fish, cut the flesh into small pieces and grind, using the finest blade of the food processor. Place in a bowl, add the egg yolks and mix well. Season and divide the mixture into 4 equal portions, shaping each into a medallion shape. Roll the medallions in the flour, very carefully shaking off the excess. Heat 3 tablespoons of oil in a skillet and brown the medallions on both sides.

Trim the scallions and cut into thin slices, then add them to the pan with the fish medallions. Cook for a few minutes. Pour the white wine over, partially evaporate it, then add the tomato passata. Season again and cook for a further 5 minutes.

Meanwhile, finely chop the parsley and 4 or 5 basil leaves. Place the fish medallions on individual plates. Spoon about one quarter of the sauce over each one, sprinkle with chopped herbs and serve immediately.

Sea bass with zucchini (top); *steamed whiting* (center); *fish medallions* (bottom)

Light Seafood Stew with Lemon

Bocconcini di mare al limone

To serve 4

3 salmon fillets

4 large squid, about ¾lb

9oz uncooked jumbo shrimp

1 shallot

olive oil

¼ cup dry vermouth

finely chopped rind of 1 lemon

Preparation and cooking time: about 40 minutes

Rinse and dry the salmon fillets and cut into bite-sized pieces.

Clean the squid, removing the ink sacs. Rinse carefully and cut the body sacs into thin strips. Rinse the shrimp, cut along the stomachs with scissors and break off the tails.

Peel and finely chop the shallot, then color it in 3 tablespoons of oil. Add the squid and cook over medium heat for about 5 minutes. Season and add the pieces of salmon and continue to cook for 6 or 7 minutes. Finally, add the shrimp and cook all the seafood for another 5 minutes.

Before removing the mixture from the heat, add the vermouth and the lemon peel. Pour the stew into a warmed serving dish, garnish with slices of tomato and celery leaves, if you wish, and serve immediately.

Baked Monkfish with Rosemary

Pescatrice al rosmarino

To serve 6

1½lb monkfish tail

fresh rosemary sprigs

olive oil

½ cup dry white wine

1 small bunch fresh parsley

Preparation and cooking time: about 40 minutes

Preheat the oven to 375°F. Rinse and dry the monkfish and place it in a flameproof baking dish. Season and add a few sprigs of rosemary. Moisten with 4 tablespoons of oil and the wine, then bake in the oven for about 25 minutes.

Meanwhile, finely chop the leaves from a branch of rosemary and the parsley. When the fish is cooked, take it out of the oven and the baking dish and keep warm. Remove the sprigs of rosemary from the cooking juices, and put in the chopped herbs. Place the dish on the stove, bring the sauce to a boil and cook for about 2 minutes.

To serve, cut a few slices from the fish and place on a platter, accompanied by the sauce. If you wish, garnish with a few tender lettuce leaves, a sprig of rosemary and half a lemon, cut into a flower shape.

Mackerel in Tomato and Vinegar Sauce

Sgombri all'aceto

To serve 4

---

4 mackerel, cleaned and gutted

---

flour for dusting

---

olive oil

---

1 small bunch fresh parsley

½ tbsp capers, well drained

¼ cup dry white wine

---

white wine vinegar

---

5 tbsp tomato passata or pureed tomatoes

Preparation and cooking time: about 30 minutes

Carefully rinse the fish inside and out and dry with paper towels. Roll the fish in the flour, lightly shaking off any excess. In a skillet, heat 3 tablespoons of oil and cook the fish over high heat until golden on both sides. Lower the heat and continue to cook for about 10 minutes. Transfer the mackerel to a serving dish and keep warm.

Wash, drain and finely chop the parsley leaves, together with the capers.

Put this mixture into the cooking juices from the fish and add the wine and 4 tablespoons of vinegar. Bring to a boil, then add the tomato passata. Season and cook for a few minutes, until the sauce has reduced slightly and thickened.

Pour this sauce over the fish and serve immediately.

Carpaccio of Salmon Trout

Carpaccio di trota

To serve 4

---

1 head young leafy lettuce

---

2 salmon trout fillets, cleaned, about 1lb 6oz

---

1 tomato

---

1 cup button mushroom caps

½ cucumber

---

4 tbsp lemon juice

Worcestershire sauce

---

fresh chives

---

extra-virgin olive oil

Preparation time: about 15 minutes, plus marinating

Carefully trim the lettuce and rinse it in plenty of water, then drain well. Make a bed of the leaves on a serving plate. Check that the trout fillets are perfectly clean then, using a very sharp knife, slice them very thinly, like smoked salmon. Arrange the slices on the bed of lettuce. Wash and dry the tomatoes and mushroom caps, and peel the cucumber. Dice all these vegetables very finely and sprinkle them over the fillets of fish.

To make the dressing, in a bowl, mix a pinch of salt with the lemon juice. Add a generous dash of Worcestershire sauce, a pinch of pepper, some snipped chives and 10 tablespoons of extra-virgin olive oil. Beat the dressing until very smooth, then pour it over the carpaccio. Cover the plate with plastic wrap, put in a cool place and leave to marinate for about 30 minutes.

Baked monkfish with rosemary (left, top); light seafood stew with lemon (left, bottom); carpaccio of salmon trout (below)

Fillets of John Dory with Lettuce and Peas

Filetti di San Pietro con lattuga e piselli

To serve 4

about 1¼lb John Dory, cod or hake fillets

flour for dusting

1 egg, beaten

4 tbsp butter

olive oil

1 cup frozen peas

2 cups shredded lettuce

Worcestershire sauce

Preparation and cooking time: about 40 minutes

Rinse the fish well, removing the skin. Dry well, then dip them first in the flour, shaking off any excess, then in the beaten egg.

In a skillet, heat the butter with 3 tablespoons of oil until very hot. Put in the fillets and cook for about 3 minutes on each side. Remove them from the pan, season and keep warm.

Meanwhile, cook the peas in boiling salted water. Put the vegetables into the cooking juices in the skillet and heat quickly, stirring with a wooden spoon. Season and add a few drops of Worcestershire sauce. Serve the fish fillets surrounded by the cooked vegetable garnish.

Fillets of Salmon au Gratin

Salmone in filetti, gratinato

To serve 6

1½lb salmon fillets

½ cup dry white wine

fresh thyme sprigs

fresh marjoram leaves

olive oil

1 shallot

1 × 14oz can chopped tomatoes

6 slices white bread

1 small bunch fresh parsley

Preparation and cooking time: about 1 hour, plus 2 hours marinating

Rinse the fillets, then remove any skin and lay them on a long, deep platter. Pour the wine over and cover thickly with sprigs of thyme and marjoram. Season and leave to marinate for about 2 hours.

Preheat the oven to 375°F. Transfer the marinated salmon fillets to a baking dish and strain and reserve the marinating liquid. Mix the liquid with 4 tablespoons of oil and pour over the fish. Cook in the preheated oven for about 25 minutes.

Meanwhile, peel and finely chop the shallot and color it lightly in 1 tablespoon of oil in a saucepan. Add the chopped tomatoes without their juices, season and cook over high heat for about 15 minutes, until the mixture has reduced and thickened.

Crumb the bread in a blender. Take the salmon fillets out of the oven and sprinkle them with the bread crumbs and a trickle of oil, then cook under a hot broiler until the bread crumbs have formed a golden crust. Transfer the fish to a warmed serving platter, scatter over some finely chopped parsley and pour the sauce over. Serve at once.

Sea Bream with Mustard Sauce

Orate alla senape

To serve 4

4 small sea bream, cleaned and gutted

fresh basil leaves

fresh rosemary leaves

1 medium onion

½ garlic clove

olive oil

⅔ cup dry white wine

a little light stock (a cube will do)

4 tbsp whole-grain mustard

Preparation and cooking time: about 40 minutes

Preheat the oven to 375°F. Wash the fish inside and out and pat dry well. Season and place a few basil and rosemary leaves inside each fish. Arrange the bream well spaced out in a flameproof baking dish. Finely chop the onion and garlic and sprinkle these over the fish. Moisten with a trickle of good olive oil.

Cook in the preheated oven for 10 minutes, then baste the bream with the wine and a ladleful of stock. Cook for another 10 or 15 minutes, then take the baking dish out of the oven and remove the fish.

Put the baking dish on the stove and bring the cooking juices to a boil. Stir in the mustard. Stir, simmering, for 1 or 2 minutes, than pour the sauce over the bream and serve.

Fillets of salmon au gratin (top); sea bream with mustard sauce (center); fillets of John Dory with lettuce and peas (bottom)

Trout with Artichokes
Trotelle con carciofi

To serve 4

4 trout, cleaned and gutted

1 fresh rosemary sprig

1 fresh sage sprig

1 fresh parsley sprig

olive oil

2 artichokes

lemon juice

2 medium onions

1 carrot

¼ cup dry white wine

Preparation and cooking time: about 40 minutes

Preheat the oven to 400°F. Rinse the fish inside and out, then dry with paper towels. Inside each fish, place a sprig of rosemary, a sage leaf and a parsley sprig. Season, then lay the trout in a baking dish, trickle a little olive oil over and cook in the oven for 10 minutes.

Trim the artichokes, removing the tough outer leaves and the spiny parts. Cut them in half and, if necessary, discard the chokes. Place the prepared artichokes in water acidulated with a little lemon juice. Peel the onions, trim, scrub and wash the carrot, then drain and dry the artichokes. Chop all the vegetables.

In a skillet, heat 3 tablespoons of oil, put in the chopped vegetables and sweat over moderate heat until tender. Moisten with the wine, bring to a boil then, before it evaporates, briefly remove the trout from the oven and pour the mixture over them.

Return the baking dish to the oven and cook for a further 15 minutes. Serve the trout straight from the dish, with all the vegetables and herbs.

Mussels with Saffron
Cozze ai pistilli di zafferano

To serve 4

2½lb mussels

olive oil

1 garlic clove

1 small red chili pepper, chopped

1 shallot

1 bay leaf

1 cup whipping cream

½ envelope of powdered saffron

1 teaspoon saffron strands, soaked for 10 minutes in 1 tbsp of water

Preparation and cooking time: about 35 minutes

Scrub the mussels, remove the beards and any impurities from the shells, then rinse thoroughly under running water. Discard any that are open.

In a large saucepan, heat 3 tablespoons of oil with a halved and lightly crushed clove of garlic and the chili pepper. Add the mussels, cover and set the pan over high heat until they open. (Discard any that do not open.) When they have opened, take the pan off the heat and remove the top shell of each mussel, leaving them still attached to the half shell. Keep warm.

Meanwhile, strain any mussel cooking liquid. Return it to the heat, add the finely chopped shallot, bay leaf, cream and powdered saffron. Cook this sauce, stirring with a wooden spoon, until thick and reduced by about half. Now add the mussels, immersing them in the sauce. Add the saffron strands, cover and cook over high heat for 5 minutes. Season then divide the mussels between individual plates and serve.

Aromatic Hake Steaks
Tranci di nasello aromatici

To serve 4

1¼lb hake or cod steaks

3 slices of white bread

½ tablespoon capers

1 sprig fresh rosemary

1 fresh sage leaf

celery leaves

2 anchovy fillets

green olive paste

olive oil

4 tbsp butter

Preparation and cooking time: about 35 minutes

Preheat the oven to 400°F. Rinse the fish and dry carefully on paper towels. Crumb the bread in a blender and transfer to a bowl. Drain and finely chop the capers, the leaves from a sprig of rosemary, a sage leaf, 3 celery leaves, and the anchovy fillets, and add these to the bowl. Stir, then add about 2 tablespoons olive paste, 3 tablespoons of oil and a pinch of salt and pepper. Stir to amalgamate all the ingredients properly, then coat the fish with the paste, pressing to make sure the steaks are completely and uniformly covered.

Heat the butter in a large skillet and brown the fish steaks on both sides, without cooking them through. Transfer the fish to a baking dish, spacing them out well, and finish cooking in the oven for about 10 minutes. Serve very hot.

Trout with artichokes (top); aromatic hake steaks (center); mussels with saffron (bottom)

Salmon and Shrimp Stew

Zuppa di scorfano e canocchie

To serve 6–8

1lb salmon fillets

½lb cooked shelled shrimp

12oz mussels

12oz clams

olive oil

2 garlic cloves

2 fresh rosemary sprigs

1 medium onion

2 celery stalks

2 carrots

½ cup dry white wine

Preparation and cooking time: about 1 hour 20 minutes

Rinse and dry the salmon fillets and shrimp. Clean the mussels and clams, removing any beards or impurities and discarding any that are open. Put the mussels and clams in separate pans, each with 2 tablespoons of oil, a chopped garlic clove and a sprig of rosemary. Cook until they are open. (Discard any that do not open.) Remove them from the pans and filter the juices through a strainer to remove any residues.

Carefully trim and chop the onion, celery and carrots, then sweat in a large saucepan with 3 tablespoons of oil until soft. Add 1 cup water and the wine and bring to a boil. Cut the salmon fillets into good-size chunks and add to the broth. Cook over medium heat, turning them only occasionally, for about 5 minutes. Carefully add in the shrimp, mussels and clams and heat through for 5 minutes. Arrange in a suitable dish and serve immediately.

Broiled Langoustines with Sweet Pepper Sauce

Grigliata di gamberoni al ragù di peperoni

To serve 4

8 langoustines

olive oil

For the sauce:

1 small onion

olive oil

½ each red and yellow bell peppers

⅓ cup pine kernels

fresh basil leaves

2 tomatoes, peeled and chopped

Preparation and cooking time: about 30 minutes

Shell the langoustines, leaving the heads on, and arrange them on a plate. Season and moisten with a trickle of olive oil. Cover the plate with another inverted plate and leave to marinate in the refrigerator for about 15 minutes.

Meanwhile, prepare the sauce. Peel and thinly slice the onion and sweat with 2 tablespoons of oil. Wash and seed the red and yellow peppers, remove the membranes and cut them into tiny dice. Add them to the pan with the onion and saute over high heat for about 2 minutes. Season, then add the pine kernels and a few rinsed and drained basil leaves, roughly torn with your hands. Cook, stirring, for about 1 minute, then put in the chopped tomatoes. Lower the heat, cover the pan and cook for about 10 minutes to reduce the sauce.

Preheat the broiler and, when it is searing hot, drain the langoustines and broil them for about 8 minutes, turning them over halfway through. As soon as they are ready, divide them between individual plates and serve piping hot, accompanied by the pepper sauce.

Salmon Trout "en Papillotte"

Trota salmonata al cartoccio

To serve 6

11oz fresh mussels

olive oil

1 garlic clove

5oz uncooked shrimp

1 shallot

1 × 7oz can chopped tomatoes

1 salmon trout, about 2¼lb, cleaned and gutted

fresh sage leaves

fresh mint leaves

fresh rosemary sprigs

1 egg white

Preparation and cooking time: about 45 minutes

Preheat the oven to 400°F. Scrub the mussels, rinse thoroughly removing any beards or impurities. Discard any that are open. Put them in a pan with 2 tablespoons of olive oil and a chopped garlic clove, cover and heat until the mussels have opened. (Discard any that do not open.) Take the pan off the heat and remove the top mussel shells, leaving the molluscs attached to the half shell. Strain any cooking juices into another pan and keep warm.

Shell the shrimp. Peel and finely chop the shallot and sweat it in a saucepan with 2 tablespoons of oil. Add the shrimp and cook over high heat until browned all over, then season with salt and pepper and moisten with the mussel juices.

Salmon trout "en papillotte" (top); grilled langoustines with sweet pepper sauce (bottom)

Bring to a boil, stir, then add the chopped tomatoes and simmer until the sauce is well thickened.

Meanwhile, rinse, dry and fillet the fish, then lay the fillets side by side on a sheet of heavy baking parchment. Finely chop a few sage, mint and

rosemary leaves and sprinkle them over the fillets. As soon as the shrimp sauce is ready, pour it evenly over the fillets, then add the mussels on their half shells and season to taste. Place another sheet of parchment over the fish, brush the edges with egg white, and seal the

package tightly. Lightly oil a cookie sheet and slide on the *papillotte*. Trickle a little oil over, then bake in the preheated oven for about 20 minutes.

Transfer the *papillotte* to a suitable platter and serve, opening it in front of the assembled company.

Macaroni with squid and sardines

Baby Octopus in Green Sauce

Moscardini al verde

To serve 4

1¾lb baby octopus

olive oil

1 garlic clove

1 medium onion

1 small bunch fresh parsley

2 pearl onions

1 cup finely chopped lettuce

juice of ½ lemon

1 tbsp green olive paste

Preparation and cooking time: about 45 minutes

Thoroughly clean the octopus, then rinse them. Heat a pan of water and, when it starts to boil, toss in the octopus and cook for about 4 minutes. Lift them out with a slotted spoon and spread them out to dry on paper towels.

In a saucepan, heat 4 tablespoons of oil. Finely chop the garlic and onion, place in the pan and add the octopus. Cover, lower the heat to moderate and cook, stirring frequently, for about 20 minutes, until the octopus are fairly dry. If the pan becomes too dry, moisten with a little water or dry white wine.

Meanwhile, wash, drain and finely chop the parsley leaves and the pearl onions. Add this mixture and the chopped lettuce to the octopus with the lemon juice and the olive paste. Stir and cook for about another 10 minutes. Transfer to a serving dish and serve immediately.

Macaroni with Squid and Sardines

Pàcchere alle seppie

To serve 4

¾lb small squid

9oz fresh sardines

11oz large ridged macaroni

1 garlic clove

fresh basil leaves

1 medium onion, peeled

olive oil

2½ cups chopped tomatoes

½ eggplant, finely diced

Preparation and cooking time: about 50 minutes

Clean the fish, leaving the squid body sacs whole if you are using them, and filleting the sardines. Cook the macaroni in the usual way, until it is *al dente*.

Meanwhile, chop the garlic, 5 basil leaves and the onion. Place in a flameproof dish with 5 tablespoons of oil and cook, uncovered, for 3 minutes. Add the chopped tomatoes, squid and finely diced eggplant. Cover and cook for 12 minutes, stirring twice. Season, add the sardines, and cook for 3 minutes.

Preheat the oven to 375°F. Grease a large baking dish with a little olive oil, put in the macaroni and mix in half the fish and sauce mixture. Cover with the remaining mixture and cook, uncovered, in the oven for 25 minutes. Leave to rest for 5 minutes before serving. If you wish, sprinkle with chopped parsley.

Seafood couscous

Seafood Couscous

Cuscusu

To serve 4

9oz small squid

9oz monkfish tail

9oz jumbo shrimp

9oz clams in their shells

2 garlic cloves

1 small bunch fresh parsley

1 small onion

olive oil

1 cup chopped tomatoes

3 cups ready-prepared couscous

Preparation and cooking time: about 1 hour

Clean the fish and shellfish and rinse carefully in cold water; chop into largish pieces. Chop the garlic, parsley and onion, and place in a large flameproof dish with 4 tablespoons of oil. Cook, uncovered, for 3 minutes. Add the chopped tomatoes, season and stir well. Cover and cook for 3 minutes. Add the squid and cook for 12 minutes, stirring at least once. Stir, add the monkfish, clams and shrimp, and cook for 8 minutes. Discard any clams that do not open. Leave to rest, covered, for 10 minutes.

Place the couscous in a large, deep dish and pour 1¼ cups lightly salted hot water over, to which you have added a tablespoon of oil. Stir and cook in the microwave for 2 minutes. Stir the couscous again and arrange the fish and its juices and sauce on top.

Cold Fish Mousse

Sformato di Pesce, Freddo

To serve 8

4 envelopes plain gelatin

4oz monkfish, cut into walnut-sized pieces

flour

butter

olive oil

½lb onions

2 garlic cloves

½lb shrimp, peeled and heads removed

½ cup dry white wine

2½ cups fish stock

Preparation and cooking time: about 40 minutes plus overnight refrigeration

Dissolve the gelatin in a little cold water. Lightly flour the monkfish pieces and cook them very gently in 2 tablespoons of butter and 2 tablespoons of olive oil, without browning them. Add a little salt and leave on a plate to cool. Finely chop the onion with the garlic and sauté in the skillet the monkfish was cooked in. Add the shrimp and brown gently, stirring from time to time with a wooden spoon. Pour over the white wine and allow to evaporate. Season with salt and pepper. Then pour in the fish stock, stir and bring slowly to the boil.

Pour the contents of the pan into a blender and leave on maximum speed for a couple of minutes. Strain the mixture into a bowl. Stir in the gelatin, mixing until you are sure it has completely dissolved. Line the bottom and sides of a 5-cup rectangular baking pan with foil. Pour in the fish purée and sink the pieces of monkfish into it. Leave to cool at room temperature, then cover with a piece of plastic wrap and refrigerate overnight. Before serving, turn out the mousse on to a dish and garnish as you please. Serve at once.

Place in the blender the anchovy fillets, olives, artichoke heart, a few leaves of parsley and the yogurt. Blend to form a smooth mixture and mix with the mayonnaise and a tablespoon of the strained cooking liquid from the shrimp. Check and adjust the seasoning to taste. Serve the salad with the dressing.

Mixed Salad

Insalata Vigorosa

To serve 4

1 large yellow bell pepper

2 skinless frankfurter sausages, cooked

3 slices ham

¼ lb tuna in oil

1 tbsp chopped parsley

1 pimiento

2 tbsp tomato ketchup

1 tbsp mustard

Worcestershire sauce

½ cup mayonnaise

Preparation time: about 40 minutes

Wash the bell pepper and cut it into strips, discarding the stalk and seeds. Place in a bowl. Thinly slice the frankfurter sausages and cut the ham into wide strips. Mix with the bell pepper. Add the well-drained and coarsely flaked tuna and stir carefully. Transfer to a serving dish and sprinkle with a tablespoon of chopped parsley.

Prepare the dressing: Place the pimiento, ketchup, mustard and a generous dash of Worcestershire sauce in the blender and blend vigorously until smooth. Mix with the mayonnaise, test and adjust the seasoning according to taste. Serve the salad with the prepared dressing.

August Delight

Delizia d'Agosto

To serve 4

1 tender heart Boston lettuce

1 tender heart Romaine lettuce

⅜ cup dry white wine

½ bay leaf

1 garlic clove

2-3 sprigs parsley

2-3 whole black peppercorns

½lb shrimp

1 cup canned yellow corn

4 radishes

2 anchovy fillets in oil

2 green olives in brine, pitted

1 artichoke heart in oil

4 tbsp plain full-cream yogurt

½ cup mayonnaise

Preparation and cooking time: about 1 hour

Pull the leaves off both lettuces, wash and drain and spread out to dry on a tea-towel.

Place on the heat a saucepan containing 2¼ cups of water, the dry white wine, half a bay leaf, a garlic clove and 2-3 sprigs of parsley. Season with a very little salt and 2-3 whole black peppercorns and bring slowly to the boil. Add the shrimp and cook for 2-3 minutes. Remove from the heat, cover the pan and leave to stand for about 10 minutes. Drain and peel the shrimp, keeping a little of the cooking liquid.

Rinse the corn under running water and spread out to dry on absorbent paper towels. Cut or break the lettuce leaves into pieces and thinly slice the radishes. Mix the corn, lettuce, radishes and shrimp in a salad bowl.

Whitebait Omelets

Tortini di gianchetti

To serve 4

7oz whitebait

4 eggs

¼ cup whipping cream

1 small bunch fresh parsley

butter

Preparation and cooking time: about 30 minutes

Preheat the oven to 350°F. Place the whitebait in a fine strainer and rinse them very carefully under cold running water. Drain thoroughly with paper towels.

Meanwhile, break the eggs into a bowl. Beat with a fork until thoroughly amalgamated, then add the cream, the finely chopped parsley leaves, and a pinch each of salt and pepper. Generously butter 4 ovenproof *cocotte* dishes and divide the whitebait evenly among them. Pour about one quarter of the egg mixture over each portion, making sure it is evenly distributed, then cook in the preheated oven for about 15 minutes. Serve immediately.

In the background of the photograph, we show a salad of whitebait, cooked briefly in lightly salted boiling water, acidulated with lemon juice and white wine, and then served tepid, dressed with olive oil, lemon juice and chopped parsley.

August delight (far left, opposite); *whitebait omelets* (left)

Aromatic Sea Bream

Dentice aromatico

To serve 4

1 sea bream, about 2½lb

chopped fresh herbs (thyme, sage, marjoram)

8 large lettuce leaves

¼lb unsmoked bacon slices

8 anchovy fillets, chopped

olive oil

1lb tomatoes

¼ cup dry white wine

Preparation and cooking time: about 45 minutes

Clean and scale the bream very thoroughly, if necessary, then rinse under running water. Dry the fish well by patting it with a double thickness of paper towels.

Season inside and out with salt, then with a pinch of chopped herbs.

Blanch the lettuce leaves in boiling water. Refresh and lay out half on a dish towel. Arrange half the bacon on top, then put on the sea bream. Cover the fish with the remaining bacon and wrap it in the rest of the lettuce leaves, to make a package.

Place the fish on a cookie sheet and scatter over the chopped anchovies, then trickle on a little olive oil. Place in the oven preheated to 425°F and cook for about 10 minutes.

Blanch the tomatoes, peel and dice them. Add the tomatoes to the fish as it cooks and sprinkle with the white wine. Season with salt and pepper.

After about 20 minutes, remove the fish from the oven. Drain well, place on a serving platter and keep warm. Rub the sauce through a food mill, then pour it over the fish. Serve the sea bream immediately, accompanied by a fresh salad.

INDEX